Suzanne's Garden Secrets

Suzanne's Garden Secrets

by

SUZANNE WARNER PIEROT

DRAWINGS BY JILL WEBER

BOBBS-MERRILL

INDIANAPOLIS / NEW YORK

LIBRARY OF CONGRESS CATALOGING IN PUBLICATION DATA

Pierot, Suzanne.

Suzanne's garden secrets.

Includes index.

1. Gardening.   I.   Title.

SB453.P54   635.9   77-15444

ISBN 0-672-52203-9

Designed by Helen Barrow
Manufactured in the United States of America

First printing

For Guin and Jacques

Contents

Preface

This is a book for growing pains.

It is filled with remedies that relieve, reduce and ease the labor of bringing life out of the ground. It is also crammed with descriptions of operations (mostly painless) that will increase the pleasure you can get from working in the soil. Or cutting and preserving a perfect bloom. Or growing a feast of vegetables and fruits so fresh and plump the juice almost bursts through the skin.

You'll find hints, ideas and strategies that will allow you to shorten your gardening chores and give you time for more gardening chores. Then, too, this book will give you a perfectly legitimate excuse (if you need one) for never throwing anything away. It will transform you from a saver into a savior. Throughout its pages you will find ways to recycle for use in the garden a great many things less fortunate *people (those who are not gardeners) throw away. It will also show you how to make good use of the food you don't eat (garbage), even if you live in an apartment.*

Scattered through the book are some ingenious ways to outsmart insects, using everything from cucumber peels and eggshells to beer. You can't help admiring the contributors of these secrets. The tremendous patience and research that brought forth so many ways to rid the garden of pests without using chemicals. Even if you are not overburdened with pesky insects, I hope you will have as much fun (and amazement) reading about the ways as I did in collecting them. You'll also find suggestions for fertilizers that use the most unlikely materials, such as dog and human hair, banana skins, saltpeter and Epsom salts.

I have tried to make this book an almanac of practical information. Each "secret" is self-contained, which means you can open the book at any page and learn something, for use in your garden or to impress anyone who will listen. Many of the secrets have been known to expert gardeners for years. Others have only recently been discovered. Some have been handed down from generation to generation, from continent to continent. Several of the best have been contributed by novice gardeners who came to gardening with a marvelous fresh perspective. I would like to express my appreciation to them and to all the wonderfully friendly people who knowingly and unknowingly shared their secrets with me: the people at garden clubs, plant societies, botanical gardens; the myriads of gardeners who wrote magazine and newspaper articles; and the many other knowledgeable garden craftsmen, farmers, professional flower growers and florists.

This book represents a lifetime of jotting down their thoughts, their advice, their experiences, along with my own. Because there is a strong, intangible bond among gardeners, it has been a most pleasurable task. Gardeners are very willing to share their knowledge. I can't think of any other group with a common bond whose members are so sincerely helpful to one another.

If I seem to be carried away with enthusiasm over many of the secrets in this book, it is because I am. Discovering a simple solution to a nagging problem is one of the great joys of my life. The feeling is catching. For starters read Chapter Two, page 54, "Keep Raccoons Out of Corn," or page 44, "Fertilizer from Your Blender."

I would also like to express my thanks to Sylvia Dowling for her tireless enthusiasm while working with me on the manuscript.

SUZANNE WARNER PIEROT
New York City, 1978

Chapter One

Planting Secrets

HOW TO RAISE MORE
THAN A CROP OF CALLUSES

OH SAY CAN YOU SEED

Planting Small Seeds, One by One

When you plant one seed to a container, and especially when you're using small peat pots, moisten the tip of a pencil, pick up each seed with it, and deposit it exactly where you want it. (Save your saliva. Use a glass of water to moisten the pencil.)

Facial Tissues Aren't Only for Noses

Often tiny seeds (such as petunia or begonia) can barely be seen by the naked eye. They can get lost in your planting mixture before they germinate, no matter how carefully you water. Even when you water from the bottom, the small seeds are pulled down by the weight of the water and are lost. Here's a secret for almost perfect germination, with no loss of seed. It's a goody. Take your planting container—the most controllable size for tiny seeds is the 5½ x 6-inch plastic or cardboard box small plants come in when you buy them at the supermarket or nursery. Fill it with vermiculite, perlite, soil or any of the many ready-made planting mixtures, and water well. Now separate a double-ply facial tissue into two sheets. Spread one of them over your wet planting mixture and scatter your seeds over it. Cover them with the other sheet of tissue. Once you've done so, don't attempt to move the tissue. Your seeds are now in their soft bed between the layers, and even if you water from the top, they cannot become lost. What's more, they will usually germinate long before the tissue dissolves. If your planting container is larger than one tissue, simply use more, but always separate them first. As you sow, so shall ye save.

Another Way to Plant Tiny Seeds

I get more suggestions for planting tiny seeds than for almost anything else. The reason, of course, is that the loss of small seeds is considerable unless extra precautions are taken. Here's an idea that may strike your fancy. Fold a piece of paper in half and shake the seeds into the fold. Hold the folded paper with one hand and slowly move it over the soil. With the other hand, tap the paper ever so gently, so that the seeds fall off one at a time.

Petunia Seeds

Here's still another way to grow tiny, tiny seeds such as petunia. Put three tablespoons of cornmeal into a paper bag and empty the package of seeds into it. Shake the bag well, and then slowly shake it out into your soil or planting mixture. This certainly spaces out the plants, but you still run the risk that water will pull the seeds so deeply into the soil that they cannot germinate. Some people swear by this method, but I like the tissue method best. Incidentally, petunias planted in front of spring bulbs hide the bulbs' dying foliage. Ageratum does too.

Covering Tiny Seeds

Most tiny seeds need no covering, but if you insist, use a small strainer and sift the soil over the seeds.

The Old Jar Trick

Some people swear by this method. Often, I swear at it, but you may not. Very tiny seeds and slow-germinating seeds develop with no loss from damping off (a fungus disease) when grown in a wide-mouth jar laid horizontally. Holding a jar on its side, put some damp sphagnum moss into it. Then sprinkle the seeds as evenly as possible on top of the sphagnum. Perforate the cover (either the real cover or

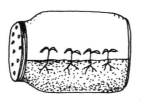

aluminum foil) to allow ventilation. Put the cover on the jar and lay it on top of the refrigerator for bottom heat. (The refrigerator top is one of the few places in your house that is constantly warm.) The condensation drips down the sides of the jar rather than on the seedlings. You can leave the jar on the refrigerator without doing another thing to it until the seeds germinate and become large enough for transplanting.

How to Germinate Hard-to-Germinate Seeds

Both hard-to-germinate and hard-coated seeds can be germinated with the greatest of ease if you do the following. Make yourself a "seed soaker," which is just a piece of an old dish towel, pillow case or what-have-you stuffed with peat moss, sawdust or sphagnum moss and stitched shut—just like a tiny sleeping bag. It should be stuffed an inch thick. After you've given it a good soaking, allow it to drain so that it is very wet but not dripping. Next, space out your seeds on top of the soaker. Then roll up your soaker very tightly. After the first week, open it daily to see if germination has started. Pot the seeds that have germinated and roll your soaker up again. Check each day until all seeds have germinated. If your soaker needs water, spray it when it is unrolled. Chances are it won't need any if the original soaking was thorough.

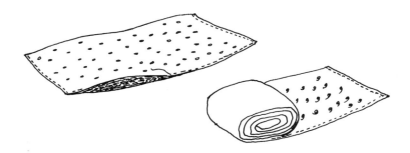

How to Start a Tree from Seed

Better to start when you're young. It takes a while, but it's fun. It's almost like giving birth. It's your very own—without you it would not be—so the sense of pride in its life can be overwhelming. Here's how you can do it faster than sowing your seed outdoors in the winter and waiting for spring before germination begins. It's a process called stratification, and all it requires is placing the seeds in your refrigerator for a specified period of time. Mix the seeds with moist sand and peat moss. Put the mixture into a mason jar or plastic container in your refrigerator for two, three, or four months, depending on the seed. Then remove and sow. Seeds that need only two months are apple, alder, ash, beech, flowering cherry, peach and pear. Four months is recommended for buckeye, butternut, Eastern red cedar, hickory, magnolia and black walnut. Now that you know how, start your own forest.

Speedy Germination for Corn

Here's how to get your corn seeds sprouting fast. Soak a towel in lukewarm water and wring it out so it won't drip. Spread your corn seeds on the towel and roll them up inside the towel. Place the towel in a pan in a warm place. Check it each day to be sure it has not dried out. If it has, sprinkle it with a little warm water. In a few days, your corn seeds will have "whiskers"—long white sprouts with tiny side hairs. These are the roots. You must handle them very carefully when you plant, but they are worth your care.

How to Know How Deep to Plant Seeds

Here's a method many gardeners swear by when planting seeds. You might call it a good rule of finger. For small seeds like radishes, plant them one-half fingernail deep. For zinnias and beets and other medium-sized seeds, plant as deep as the base of your fingernail. For medium-large seeds—the size of a pea—plant one-half the distance between the first joint and the fingernail. Beans, nasturtiums and other seeds their size should be planted all the way down to the first joint of your index finger. Always delighted to "point" the way.

Use Your Refrigerator for Heat

Touch the top of your refrigerator and you'll find that it's warm. It's always that way, in case you've never spent time touching the tops of refrigerators. Well, it is the ideal spot for the germination of seeds. Unless you buy heating cables, there is no better place to put your seed tray. You'll be amazed at the speed of germination with the gentle bottom heat your nice cold "fridge" provides.

Using Heat for Speedy Germination

There are a few seeds that must have cold in order to germinate, and it's always specified on the seed package, but the majority need heat. If you'll make a weak solution of manure (almost a manure tea) and soak your seeds in it, you'll find that the manure's heat will hasten the germination. I'm told that in Italy, whole ripe olives are fed to the turkeys; their seeds germinate faster after they have passed through the birds' digestive tracts. Nature works in wondrous ways. Did you ever notice how quickly a forest reseeds itself after a fire? Suddenly there are thousands of seedlings rising from the ashes. They come from seeds brought to the forest by animals and birds through the years. It took the fire's heat to break their hard, thick coats and thus cause germination.

Freeze Iris Seeds

Iris seeds are slow to germinate. Here's a cool idea to help them get going. Freeze the seeds by putting them into an ice-cube tray half filled with water. When the water is frozen, add more water to the tray and freeze for about four weeks. Then plant the seeds, ice cubes and all.

How to Water Seeds Without Watering

Make drainage holes in a 6-inch pie or cake pan and set it in an 8-inch pie or cake pan. Put soil in the 6-inch pan and sow seeds in it. Put at least an inch of sphagnum moss in the larger pan around the smaller pan. Fill the larger pan with water and keep the moss damp at all times, so that the soil in the seed pan will always be wet without your ever watering it.

Planting Rules

Always remember, whether you start your seed indoors or out, the soil temperature is more important than the amount of moisture in it. Most seeds will germinate in soil that is bone-dry, even though that soil would not support a seedling. Therefore, rule one: always make sure your soil is warm; and rule two: once the seedlings appear, make sure the soil never dries out.

What to Do When You Want More Garden Than
You Have Space For

You don't have to have a lot of space in order to have a big garden if you grow your plants in layers—in a pyramid shape. Make your layers out of old railroad ties, as the illustration shows. Fill each tier, one at a time, with soil. Water and let the soil settle before you start your next tier. With railroad ties, you can do the entire pyramid in 100 square feet. Some nurseries and seed companies sell ready-made pyramids. Look in your seed catalogs.

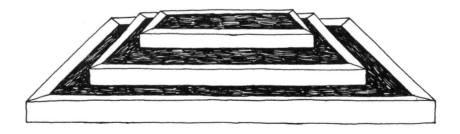

Your County Agent Has a Lot of Answers

Get to know the phone number of your county agricultural agent or agricultural experiment station. Either can be a great help when you need information about tree or plant diseases, sprays, soil testing, and the average date of the last killing frost in your area. That last bit of information is pure gold to anyone setting out plants that cannot withstand even a touch of frost. Look in the telephone book under "U.S. Government." If it isn't in the book, call your congressman's local office.

THE EVERYTHING-MAKES-A-GOOD-SEED-CONTAINER DEPARTMENT

Containers for Peat Pots That Are as Cheap as Dirt

To contain those marvelous peat pots while growing lovely things in them, cut a milk carton in half lengthwise and you'll have two ideal containers. You can also use the plastic and aluminum trays that meat, cottage cheese and TV dinners come in. Be sure to punch a few holes in them for drainage.

More D.T.A.A. (Don't Throw Anything Away)

I get so many ideas for seed containers from all over the country. Here are the latest: cut-down bleach jugs, pudding and whipping bowls, and plastic ice-cream containers. But again, always punch a few drainage holes in anything you use to germinate seeds or to hold cuttings.

Another No-Cost Container

Save your egg cartons; and plant 1 seed in each of the 12 compartments, but transplant them as soon as the second set of leaves appears.

Coffee Cans for Seed Starters

Coffee cans with plastic lids are also excellent for starting seeds. Cut off the metal top and bottom. Punch some drainage holes in the plastic lid, and put it on the bottom of the can. Fill the can with soil, and plant your seed. When the plant is large enough to transplant, you simply remove the plastic lid and push.

Make Your Own Mini-Greenhouse at No Cost

Want a greenhouse for your seedlings? Want to hasten germination of your precious seeds? Cut off the bottom of a clear plastic gallon milk, bleach or fabric softener bottle or carton—after you've washed it carefully, of course. Unscrew the cap (for ventilation) and place the bottle over your seed or seedling box. This works even better outdoors in early spring. If you place it right on the soil over tender seedlings, you will never have to worry if a quick frost shows up. Just put the cap back on the bottle on really cold nights.

Yep. Even Medicine Cups

Those one-ounce plastic medicine cups also make great containers for seedlings. Be sure to burn a hole in the bottom for drainage. Hold a needle over a match until it gets hot. Then push it through the cup to make your tiny hole.

Tin Cans for Starter Pots

Start your own recycling "plant." Cut out both the top and the bottom of a tin can with a can opener. Crimp the bottom of the can in several places. Then take one of the lids and drop it into the can, pushing it down as far as it will go. Now you've got a starter pot complete with drainage.

Turn Berry Baskets into Plant Pots

Those plastic berry baskets you get at the supermarkets can be used for a number of things besides holding berries. Use them for temporary pots, or for plants you're going to give away. Line the inside with cheesecloth or a cut-up nylon stocking. Fill with soil and plant.

Keep Your Pot Soil in Your Pot (Secret Number One)

If you don't have pebbles, stones, or broken clay pots to place on the bottom of your pot for drainage and for keeping the soil from washing away, use plastic window screening over the hole. It's easy to cut with ordinary scissors. It's flexible, it will not rot or rust, and you will need only two-inch squares. The soil will hold the squares in place. The screening will also keep out the insects if you put your pot on the ground outdoors. A yard of plastic screen will yield 324 two-inch squares that can be reused. You can use aluminum screening, but it costs more and is hard to cut with scissors.

Keep Your Pot Soil in Your Pot (Secret Number Two)

A rolled-up ball of nylon stocking also provides perfect drainage in flower pots and keeps the soil from washing away (nylon stockings last longer in the pot than they do on your legs). In a pot where the holes are on the side, cover the entire bottom with nylon, and extend it up the sides to cover the holes. Put the soil in the center of the pot first, then spread it out to the edges. For larger pots, wrap sphagnum moss in the stockings and shape them like balls. That way you'll get bulk without using up all your old nylons.

What Not to Use to Grow Plants In

Don't ever—no never—use a cigar box to start seedlings. This is especially true for tomatoes and eggplants. While the garden brains aren't sure about other plants as yet, it's better to play it safe and leave the cigar boxes for the trash men.

Found: A Use for Plastic Knives

I have often thought that the most useless item in today's plastic world is the plastic knife. It can't cut anything worth a darn. It can't spread anything heavier than butter, and if the butter is cold, forget it. Well, I've found a use for it. It makes a great plant labeler, indoors or out. Print out the name of the plant with a name-tape printer, press it on the handle of the knife, and push the blade into the soil. *Voilà!* A permanent marker.

Another No-Cost Idea for Planters

Save your eggshells as well as your egg cartons for seeding. The only problem is cracking the egg. Try to crack it neatly in half. This can be difficult when you're cooking and your mind is on other things, but if you can manage to remember neatness in cracking, you can use each half of the shell as a tiny pot for your seeds (poke a hole in each eggshell bottom with a needle for drainage before you fill it with soil). The egg carton will hold a dozen half shells neatly in place. When you're ready to plant the seedling outdoors, give the shell a farewell squeeze (enough to crack it) and put it in the soil. There will be no transplant shock, and the eggshell will eventually fertilize your plant.

WHEN THE SEEDLINGS EMERGE

How to Transplant Seedlings with Loving Care

Remember the old-fashioned pens with removable pen points? If you have any or can lay your hands on some, get them. They make great seedling pluckers. Separate the tips of the pen points and you will be able to pluck out those delicate seedlings like a mother bird caring for its young.

Ice Cream Scoop for Transplanting

Try an ice cream scoop next time you're transplanting seedlings. Especially those with lots of roots. Very handy, indeed.

A LITTLE LIGHT ON BULBS
AND OTHER ILLUMINATING FACTS

How to Transplant Growing Bulbs in the Spring

Most people swear you cannot move narcissus, tulips or daffodils after they have started in the spring. I disagree. If you dig a clump with a spading fork, place it in a pail with a little cold water in the bottom, carry it that way to its new site, and put it in a hole larger than the clump, you'll have no trouble. Drop a trowelful of aged manure into the new hole before you plant the clump; then tamp down and water well, and your plant will not only survive but thrive.

How to Keep Rodents from Eating Tulip Bulbs

Plant daffodils near or around your tulips. Daffodil bulbs are poisonous to most rodents—but what a lovely way to die.

How to Economize When You Naturalize

The custom when planting spring bulbs is to throw a trowelful of bone meal into the planting hole. But if you are naturalizing and planting hundreds or thousands of bulbs, this can run into a tremendous amount of money. Bone meal is very expensive these days. Less expensive and almost as good is superphosphate. For every thousand bulbs, sprinkle 100 pounds into the soil before planting.

Never Forget This About Bulbs

If you can't remember anything else about the planting of bulbs, remember this: they will tolerate almost any soil, but their roots must never be allowed to stand in water, or they will rot. Drainage must be good or your bulbs won't be.

Keep Bulbs from Rotting in the Ground

If your soil is inclined to be damp, dig bulb holes an inch deeper than necessary and put an inch of sand into the hole before planting the bulb.

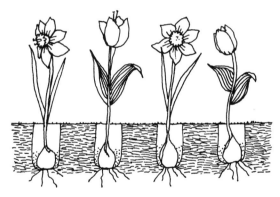

Food for Bulbs

Bulbs need a good amount of phosphorus and potash. These two nutrients give them the ability to develop beautiful flowers with strong stems and to grow firm, heavy bulbs the following season. Bone meal will give them the phosphorus they need. Wood ashes—plain, ordinary wood ashes from your fireplace—will provide a rich source of potash.

VOIDING THE VARMINT

How to Discourage Mice, Moles, Chipmunks and Squirrels from Eating Tulip Bulbs

These little pests love tulip bulbs, but if you plant daffodils, narcissus, small grape hyacinths or scilla in bands around your tulips, you stand a good chance of saving your tulip bulbs, inasmuch as these rodents do not like the taste of the above-mentioned beauties. Planting a mothball next to a tulip bulb at planting time will discourage the rodents for one season anyway. Sometimes it helps to scatter the mothballs over the area where established tulips are planted.

Another Way to Deter Moles

There's a marvelous spring bulb—related to the lily family—that for some reason will deter moles. It's the Grand Imperial *Fritillaria,* a very stately plant which grows about 3 feet high and bears yellow, orange-red or red flowers in clusters on the tops of the stems. Deterring moles is only one of its many virtues, and it deserves a place in your spring garden. Plant the bulbs in autumn, at the same time as tulips.

Protect Crocus from Rabbits

Plant crocus close to the stems of low-growing deciduous shrubs to give them a buffer from those hungry rabbits.

Berry Baskets for Bulbs

Those plastic berry baskets you get at the supermarket make great underground cages to hold bulbs. Put your bulbs in them when planting. The varmints will find it difficult, if not impossible, to eat them. Your bulbs planted this way will also end up as plants perfectly spaced.

How to Plant Iris—or, When Iris Eyes Are Smiling

What you don't do is just dig a hole and put in the iris. What you do do is to scoop out two shallow holes, leaving a ridge between them. The iris rhizome (the root) sits on the ridge, and the feeding roots are spread out in holes on either side. If a little dirt falls on top of the rhizome, don't worry about it. If you'll remember that the iris plant travels in the direction of the growing end, you'll have a better-looking clump. Always plant three rhizomes in a clump.

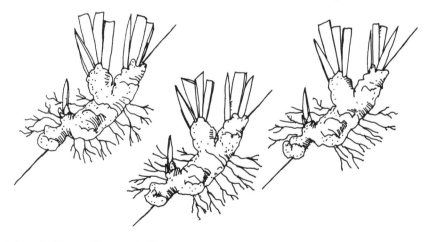

How to Grow Crocus in Your Lawn

There's something very whimsical about crocus springing up in the middle of a lawn. If you want a natural effect, the way to do it is to cut out pieces of sod, plant the bulbs 2 inches deep, and then replace the sod. But once the crocus are up, don't mow the lawn until the leaves have withered, or you won't get any flowers the next spring. Usually, by the time the lawn needs mowing, the crocus are gone. That's Nature's plan anyway, but sometimes she slips up.

GARDENING, LIKE POLITICS, MAKES STRANGE BEDFELLOWS

The Meaning of Companion Planting

It doesn't mean you're going to plant a friend. It does mean a matching of plants that help one another. For example, a marigold is a companion plant to a rose because it helps the rose by deterring Japanese beetles. Any plant that can repel, trap or deter insects or that can support, shade or share space with another is a companion plant.

How Companion Planting Works

Thanks to modern science, we now know how companion planting works. After exhaustive testing, it was found that insects are confused as well as repelled by the barrage of chemical odors emitted by the plant they like along with the plant they don't like. An aphid loves a rose, but he becomes confused by both the rose odor and that of an onion companion plant grown nearby. Says Cornell's prestigious College of Agriculture, "The confusion of chemical stimuli offered by a mixture of plants can cause the breakdown of an insect's orientation, feeding habits and population numbers." Thank goodness. We'd be up to our nostrils in insects if this didn't happen.

Making Companion Planting Work

When you're using one plant as an insect deterrent for another, you've got to plant it fairly close to the one you're protecting. The best way to do it is in zigzag rows. For instance, if you want onions to protect beets, zigzag your onions and beets in two rows.

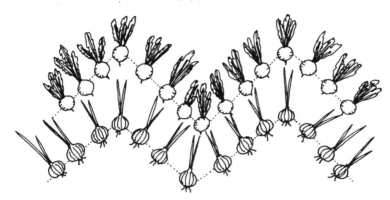

Getting Rid of Insects Naturally

The trick is to find the enemy plant and plant it near the flower or vegetable that is being molested. Here's a list of insects you want to keep away from vegetables and flowers and the companion plant that will help turn them away.

TO REPEL	FROM	GROW
asparagus beetles	asparagus	tomatoes
aphids	broccoli	nasturtiums
aphids and Japanese beetles	roses	geraniums, chives, parsley, garlic
aphids	lettuce	chives
cucumber beetles	cucumber	marigolds
chinch bugs	any plant	onions

More Plants That Discourage Insects

Tansy repels mosquitoes. Thyme deters cabbage worm. Rosemary restrains the cabbage moth from chewing foliage. Mint discourages ants from patios, and cabbage moths from laying eggs. Marigolds (the old-fashioned kind that smell) repulse nematodes, bean beetles and Japanese beetles. Garlic, onions, chives and leeks restrain mice, moles, Japanese beetles and aphids. Basil absolutely nauseates mosquitoes and flies. Pot some and put them near your sitting areas. Painted daisy is a source of many insecticides. Grown in your garden, it will check aphids, besides looking very pretty. Geraniums, especially white ones, attract Japanese beetles from other plants. Then when they get near, the geranium odor stuns them, and that's when you can pick them up and destroy them. Plant those geraniums near your rose-bushes.

Camomile, the Plant "Doctor"

It wasn't too long ago that camomile tea was a cure-all for just about every known illness. This herb is also good for plants. When it is placed near a sick plant, the plant often recovers. Cabbages particularly seem to thrive when grown near camomile. Try it.

Foxglove, Another Plant "Doctor"

When lovely foxglove is grown near other plants, it seems to stimulate those plants' growth and longevity. I'm told by my farmer friends that potatoes and other root vegetables store better if they have been grown near foxglove. There's a lot of lore attached to this lovely old plant, and it's certainly worth considering. When foxglove's stately blooms are used in arrangements, the other flowers seem to last longer. And if tea made from foxglove leaves is put into the water for floral arrangements, the flowers seem to last longer.

Life begins the day you start a garden.

CHINESE PROVERB

Chapter Two

Growing Secrets

HOW TO AVOID WORKING
FROM DAYBREAK TO BACK BREAK

**WHEN YOU WANT YOUR
BLOOMERS TO SHOW**

Secret for Successful and Superb Chrysanthemums

They need full sun and rich soil with lots of humus, compost or rotted manure. Every spring, replant by taking small clumps from the outside of the main clump (discard the main clump). Prune by pinching tips when plants are 6 inches high, taking off about 1 inch of the tip of each stem. Do this again when the stems are 9 inches long. Pinching is very important for a beautiful bushy plant, so don't forget to do it. Feed plants in August with liquid manure or 5-10-5 fertilizer.

Secret for Successful and Superb Dahlias

Mix superphosphate (half a trowelful) with soil before setting tubers in a sunny location in a well-drained soil. Place each tuber flat, with its little eye 6 inches below the level of the ground. After the first hard frost, cut stems almost to ground level and dig up the tubers. Set them in the sun to dry. Store over the winter in dry sand or peat moss in a cool, dry place. Plant again in the late spring.

Secret for Successful and Superb Michaelmas Daisies

This perennial aster should be fed with any good garden fertilizer every two weeks for magnificent flowers. Pinch back or cut the tall varieties in early June and again in mid-July to about half their height. Cut all varieties to the ground in October.

Secret for Successful and Superb Day Lilies

The secret to growing superb day lilies in either sun or partial shade is to leave them alone. They are undemanding. Fertilize when you plant them, and leave them alone for eight to ten years, fertilizing them when you think about it. Day lilies are a delight— lovely and no work. (What other plant needs transplanting only after eight or ten years?)

Secret for Successful and Superb Delphinium

Divide when clumps have more than five flowering stalks. Feed in early spring with bone meal. When cutting, cut center flower first. Only when the flowers fade on the side branches should you cut the stalk to ground level. In October, cut the entire plant to ground level.

How to Be an Instant Garden Expert

First, guess. Guess what is the most popular flower in the world. That should be easy. It's the rose. Now, here's the hard one. What's the second most popular garden flower in the world? Would you believe the gladiolus? That's what England's Royal Horticulture Society says.

Care of Gladiolus in Colder Climates

If you want to make sure nothing will happen to your gladiolus corms, dig them out before frost is predicted. (If you care, botanically speaking, a corm is similar to a bulb, but without any scales.) They are not hardy. The most prudent care is to dig them up while the foliage is still attached. If you wait until the foliage dies, you may not be able to locate them.

Secret for Successful and Superb Gladiolus

When you plant corms, put some superphosphate in the bottom of each hole. Cut flowers when the two bottom ones begin to open. Leave the leaves on plants when you cut the flowers. The corms need them for developing for the next year. When foliage turns yellow, lift out the corms and store in peat moss in a cool, dry place.

How to Make Hydrangea Blue or Pink

Take your pick. If you want blue hydrangea flowers, you must keep the soil very acid. The pH should be 5.5 or lower. You can get it that way with an acid fertilizer or a constant mulch of oak leaves. Some people stick a few rusty nails into the soil to do it. Pink flowers come from a more alkaline soil with a pH of 6.75. A touch of limestone will do it. A touch. Not much.

What You Should Know About Peonies

These lovely old-fashioned flowers seemed to go out of style during the "flower children" era in the no-class sixties. But now, in the seventies, they are in fashion again and thoroughly appreciated by all those who grow them, discover them, and smell them. The fragrance of peonies is one of the most delightful aromas your garden can offer. Once established, peonies will last a lifetime—and then some. They get few diseases and are practically carefree, if you follow a few rules. Plant them any time in September or October, the earlier in September the better. The site is the all-important secret to good bloom. It should be in full sun. Peonies will tolerate shade half a day but at the expense of lovely, large blooms. Don't plant where peonies have grown before or near a black walnut tree. The soil should be rich and should drain well. Use plenty of compost, a handful of superphosphate, a cup of bone meal and a cup of wood ashes in the hole at planting. And remember, as you plant, this is forever, because peonies do not take well to transplanting or dividing.

How to Tell the Right Side of a Peony

The peony root has eyes like those on a potato. Be sure the eyes are on the top when planting.

The Care and Feeding of a Peony

Feed peonies every spring with bone meal. If you want really big flowers, remove the side buds. After they have flowered, always remove the blooms to the first pair of leaves below the flower head. Botrytis, a fungus carried by ants, is one of the few peony diseases, and it can be cured by spraying with Bordeaux mixture (you can buy it at your garden shop). The fungus usually can be prevented by removing any diseased foliage as soon as you see it. Burn it. Don't, for heaven's sake, throw it into the compost—it will infect your compost. In the fall, just before frost, cut the foliage of the entire plant down to ground level. Do this every year and your chances are excellent for disease-free peonies. Do grow them. They are a most satisfying and beautiful flower. And oh, that fragrance!

Secret for Successful and Superb Phlox

Phlox will live very well in either full sun or light shade as long as the soil is rich and it gets plenty of water. You must divide clumps every third year. In July and August, cut off the dead flower heads as quickly as they die so that no seeds can form. Cut the plant down to 6 inches above the ground in October.

Plants That Grow Under Adverse Conditions

Two of the toughest plants that grow in the sun are lantana and marigold. They thrive in direct sunlight and can cope with little watering, dry weather, red clay soil and not much love. But give them the latter, and wow!

Snapdragons

Snapdragons don't like an acid soil. If your soil is acid, put some lime into it. But the most important snapdragon secret is to pinch them when they are young and keep on pinching them until you have very strong, neat, bushy plants. Don't forget, snaps adore full sun.

Ageratum

To make a stunning border of ageratum, crowd the plants together. If you plant them about 6 inches apart and grow them in full sun, you'll get a continuous colorful border.

Nasturtium

Sow nasturtiums where they are to grow. Or start them in peat pots and plant them pot and all. Nasturtiums loathe being transplanted.

How to Have More and More Poinsettias

First, you must live in a climate where poinsettias grow outdoors all year long. To get more blooms, prune, prune, prune. Cut back the growing stems about every two months during the summer, and then give them another pruning—a severe one—when the plants are through blooming. Leave no more than two buds on each short stem. The canes that you have cut off after the blooming season can be used to make new plants. Stick them in the ground and keep them moist. The following year you'll have more beautiful poinsettias.

TIPS ON WATERING AND NOT WATERING AND PERSUADING SOIL TO TAKE WATER

When Not to Water Plants

Never water your plants in the hot sunshine, especially when there are chemicals in the water. The leaves will burn. The little drops act as a magnifying glass. The sun burns holes in the leaves, and you become an instant arsonist.

How to Make Watering Go a Long Way

If you want to water a plant slowly and you don't want to take the time to do it, get a one-gallon polyethylene milk container and make a tiny hole in its bottom. Tiny—no larger than a pinhole. Then fill it with water and put it on the soil. Slowly but surely the water will trickle down deep into the roots. This is an ideal way of watering a plant that needs to be watered daily.

How to Test for Proper Drainage

Dig a hole about 18 inches deep and fill it with water. If the water is still in the hole after 36 hours, the drainage is not good enough for planting anything.

How to Tell When the Ground Is Too Wet for Planting in the Spring

Simply take a handful of soil and squeeze it into a ball. If it sticks like a mud ball, the ground is too wet for planting. When a handful of soil squeezed does not form a ball but is soft and crumbly, the ground is ready for working.

How to Irrigate Clay Soil

Clay soil takes forever to absorb water. The secret to growing in clay soil is to water from below the level of the ground rather
than from the ground level. And the secret to doing that is to gather
as many empty quart juice or coffee cans as you can find. Punch about
30 to 40 holes around the entire can to within 2 inches from the bottom. Sink the cans into the ground, making sure the open top is level
with the ground. Plant seeds, seedling or established plants near the
cans. Fill your cans with water. The water will seep into the ground
and give your plant roots the water they need to thrive. You can also
fertilize this way by using a fertilizer that dissolves in water.

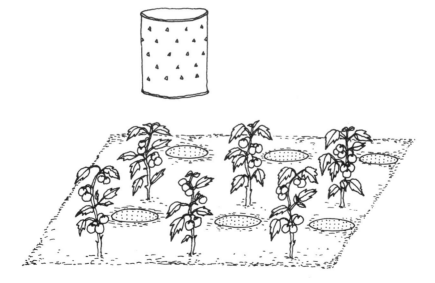

How to Conquer Hardpan Soil

Grow cowhorn turnips. After they are killed by cold, their long roots will break down, leaving long drainage holes which will allow the water to soak in.

HANDLING MAIL-ORDER PLANTS

Pot-Grown Nursery Plants

Many plants are sold in the same tin container in which they were grown. Unfortunately, the result is a tight, tenacious root ball. To grow a healthy plant, you've got to break up that mass of roots. Do it the way that seems easiest to you. Bang it, bounce it—anything to loosen it. Once you do this, you can be almost certain the plant will have a long, healthy life. If you don't, the plant may not die immediately, but it will live only two or three years. Roots need space to survive. They cannot remain cramped.

Why Bare-Root Plants Are a Better Buy

They're cheaper, for one, much less expensive than plants delivered in containers. But the real reason is they often have a better root system, because they were not grown in a cramping container. However, you must give bare-root plants special treatment after they are delivered. A bath, to be exact. Fill a tub with water. Shake off the packing material, prune broken roots, cut back the tops if needed, and then put the entire plant into the water and let it soak for 24 hours. This is a life saver for your plant, because most bare-root plants are dug in the fall and spend the winter in a refrigerated shed, with their roots exposed. After a day's soaking the plant will be ready to go into the ground, safe and sound.

When You Can't Plant Bare-Root Mail-Order Plants Immediately

The instructions you get with your mail-order plants tell you to soak the roots for 24 to 48 hours before planting. But what if you can't plant until four or five days after the plants arrive? If you're not able to heel in the plants, change the water every second day. They'll live if they get enough oxygen. Water older than 48 hours does not have enough oxygen to sustain the plants. When you keep roots in oxygen-poor water, you can suffocate them. However, don't let this secret go to your head and make you lazy. If you keep roots in water longer than ten days, other disastrous things will happen to your new bare-root plants.

FROM THE NEVER-FORGET-IT DEPARTMENT

Don't Mulch Tall Annuals

Mulching makes them set shallow root systems, which may pop out in heavy rains or during a strong windstorm.

When You Use Grass Cuttings as a Mulch

Freshly cut grass makes an easy-to-apply mulch for your vegetables or flowers. So do sawdust and fresh hay, but all rob the soil of nitrogen, and your plants will suffer the consequences. Just apply a fertilizer high in nitrogen over the ground before applying the mulch. The first number on a fertilizer, remember, is the nitrogen content. The higher, the better. A good lawn fertilizer is 12-6-4.

Economical Way to Use Bark Chips

Bark chips are great for mulching and holding down weeds, but they do cost money. One way to use fewer chips is to place the plastic bag the chips come in around the plant you're trying to protect from weeds; you can also use plastic cleaning bags. *Then,* pour the chips over the bag, just enough to cover it. That way you won't have any weeds, and your bark chips will go a longer way.

HOW TO BE A GOOD PROVIDER

Fertilizer from Your Blender

Don't throw away your vegetable parings, lettuce leaves, carrot and potato peels, orange, lemon and grapefruit rinds, eggshells, pea pods, etc. Throw them into your electric blender and turn them into liquid. Then pour into the soil around your outdoor plants. They'll literally eat it up.

Another Fertilizer from Your Blender

Save your fish scraps, put them in the blender when you have a lot, and make a fish emulsion out of them. Freeze it in an ice-cube tray, and when you're ready to fertilize your plants, throw a "fish" cube into your plant water.

Feed Bananas to Your Roses

Some of the wildest ideas are often the most sensible. This one is a good example. Banana skins have a lot of potash in them. Roses like potash. So, grind up banana skins in your meat grinder and work the gooky mess into the soil around your roses. Result—magnificent roses.

Chicken Bones for Fertilizer

As I keep saying—don't throw away anything, because it might be of use in your garden. Chicken bones, for example, turn into bone meal faster than most other bones. If you plant them two to three inches away from the base of your roses or other favorite plant, they will eventually turn into fertilizer, and until they decompose they will channel water faster to the roots of your plant.

What to Do When Plants Need Extra Food

Every once in a while, some expert advises you to give your plant extra nitrogen or phosphorus or potash in order to attain a certain effect. For instance, when your begonias have really beautiful, lush leaves but no flowers, you'll be instructed to give them more phosphorus and potash. There always seems to be something you need to do with a plant to make it produce better. Here's a good formula to follow when plants need extra nitrogen: mix one tablespoon of nitrate of soda in a gallon of water. For more phosphorus, mix 1¼ tablespoons of superphosphate in a gallon of water. For extra potash, stir two to three tablespoons of wood ashes (from your fireplace) into a gallon of water.

Richer Soil Without Compost

If you have no room for a compost pile, bury the chopped-up vegetable and fruit peelings, coffee grounds, tea leaves, etc., in the ground next to the plants you want fertilized. In time they will enrich your soil, but of course not so fast as they would if you ground them in your blender.

Keep Walnut Leaves out of Compost

Walnut leaves give off a toxic substance which I'm told is poisonous to fruit trees, grain crops and tomatoes. For that reason, don't throw walnut leaves into your compost or use it for mulch.

Hair as a Fertilizer

Hair is very rich in nitrogen. In fact, it's far richer in nitrogen than manure is. Six to seven pounds of human hair contain a pound of nitrogen—as much as in 100 to 200 pounds of manure. If you can't get his or her hair, dog hair will do just as well (dogs are human, too). Ask your local dog clipper to save you the clippings. You would look a little strange spreading hair on your lawn, but you don't use the hair that way. You dig it under when you're starting a new lawn.

PLANTERS

Sewer Pipes for Planters

If you have a friend who's a sewer engineer or contractor, you might charm him into giving you some leftover sewer pipes, or you can purchase them from a masons' supply house. They make magnificent planters.

How to Plant in a Strawberry Jar

Strawberry jars or tubs are very attractive in any garden and can be used to grow not only strawberries but flowers too. The smaller ones can be used indoors for a really fantastic, different kind of decoration. Unless you take the proper steps before you put your soil into the jar, you'll drown some of the plants when watering them and keep others from getting any moisture. Or you'll make a mess trying to water each "lip." The proper way to prepare a strawberry jar is simple. Before you put in a thimbleful of soil, make a tube out of old screening and stand it in the center of the jar. Fill the tube with

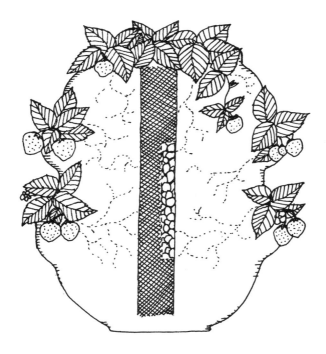

gravel. Now add the soil, a layer at a time, and place the plants in position each time the soil reaches a lip. After the jar is filled and each lip is planted, pour water into the gravel. It will filter down and be distributed evenly throughout your jar.

JOYCE KILMER WAS WRONG!
YOU, TOO, CAN MAKE A TREE

Foolproof Way to Plant a Tree

Ever hear of putting gravel columns in the ground next to your new tree? There's hardly a chance you'll lose a new tree if you do so. After you've dug your hole large enough for the tree roots to fit into comfortably, insert a cardboard tube on either side of the root area, or against the soil ball if the tree is balled. Fill your hole but don't let any soil get into those cardboard tubes. When the planting is completed, fill the tubes with coarse gravel. They will eventually decay, but the gravel columns will remain, allowing you to pour plenty of water and fertilizer into them so the roots are kept moist and well fed. The growth of your tree will be fantastic.

A Newly Planted Tree Should Be "Babied" for Four Years

Contrary to belief, you must pay special attention to any 10-foot or higher newly planted tree for about four years. The main thing is to water it thoroughly. Except in fall and winter, a good soaking is needed every two weeks, because most trees cannot establish a large enough root system in less than four years. This is particularly true when the tree is planted in a lawn. It and the lawn are competing for available moisture. They both need your help.

How to Be an Instant Garden Expert

You may already know that in Japanese the word "bonsai" used to be *hachi-no-ki*, which means "potted tree"—a trained tree growing in a pot. The word "bonsai" was devised to distinguish the trained tree growing in a pot naturally from a tree trained some other way. A bonsai is not a bonsai if it isn't grown in a pot.

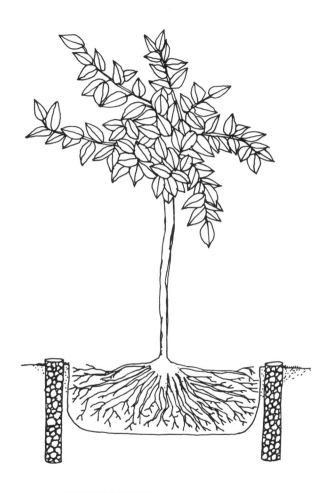

FOOLPROOF WAY TO PLANT A TREE

ADVICE TO THE LOVELAWN

Moss in Lawn

It has always been thought that the reason moss grows in some lawns is that the soil is sour—overly acid. Actually, it is more likely to be caused by poor drainage or not enough sunlight.

How to Tell Whether Your Lawn Gets Enough Water

Growing lawns require one inch of water per week. Lawn sprinklers, if they are working correctly, put out about a quarter of an inch of water per hour. Don't rely on them. Place a couple of tin cans unobtrusively around your lawn and keep them there. That way you can measure exactly how much water per week your lawn is getting from rain or watering. Don't forget to empty the cans weekly.

What to Do with Ground Where Grass Won't Grow

You can't make grass grow under some trees because the roots are too near ground level. This is especially true (and annoying) under maple trees. A neat idea is to put gravel under the tree to give it a very spiffy, clean appearance. White gravel works superbly. Just don't forget to put black plastic sheeting over the ground before you put down the gravel. This will keep weeds from growing through the gravel. Also make a few tiny holes in the plastic to allow water to get to the roots of the trees.

THE LITTLE DASTARDS

How to Get Rid of Slugs

Insecticides cannot be used around vegetables, but beer can be. Who ever heard of a drunken carrot? Dig a hole just large enough to hold a saucer or a shallow can. Fill the saucer or can with beer at nighttime. The next morning the beer should be filled with slugs, and vice versa. Repeat each evening. Cover the beer during the day if no slugs showed up the night before.

Or: yeast is pretty good for killing slugs, and it's a lot cheaper than beer. Use one tablespoon of flour and ⅛ teaspoon of yeast in a cup of water. Put the mixture into a can or saucer and sink it into the ground.

Or: try ringing the area you want protected with sand, ashes, lime or salt. If you use salt, be careful. Don't get it too close to the plants, or it will kill them.

Or: try grapefruit rinds. Set the rinds face down on the ground, like igloos. The slugs can't resist the odor, which lasts for two to three days. Check your igloos several times a day and grab the slugs while you can get them.

Become an Instant Garden Expert

Throw facts like this around: the reason slugs do so much damage is that each of them has 8,500 teeth: 85 teeth in one row, and 100 rows of teeth. That would be a bonanza for dentists, except that slugs don't have any money. Just slugs.

How to Get Rid of Spider Mites

This secret comes to us by courtesy of the Indiana Nut Growers Association. Spider mites are nasty little things, and I do mean little. It takes 50 of them to make a line an inch long! Anyway, try this method on them. Use ½ cup of buttermilk and 4 cups of wheat flour mixed in 5 gallons of water. Strain the mixture through cheese-cloth and spray on your plants. This should destroy a very high percentage of the mobile forms of mites, as well as their eggs.

Another Way to Discourage Mites

If you work in a greenhouse, you can discourage mites with the clothes you wear. According to the gardeners at the Department of Agriculture—and they ought to know—if you wash your clothes in soap-suds to which anise oil has been added, it will do the trick.

More from the U.S.D.A.

The United States Department of Agriculture also has a recipe for killing mites which you may want to try. Coriander oil in a water-emulsion spray at a two-percent ratio will kill them.

How to Get Rid of Ants

Would you believe that ants do not like cucumber peels? Grind up the peels and scatter them wherever the ants congregate. Ants don't like cleaning powder, bone meal, black pepper or white vinegar, either, but cucumber peels are best because they don't cost you any money.

How to Get Rid of Webworms

"Webworms" is a general name for all those little caterpillars that work under a silken web on trees. For webworms, nail a rag to one end of a long pole. Dip the rag into kerosene and simply wipe the rag across the web. A whoosh will do it.

How to Get Rid of Grasshoppers

Grasshoppers sleep at night, so wait until dark and go hunting with flashlight and jar. If you don't like to touch them, use kitchen tongs to pick them off branches. They're light sleepers, so don't shake the plants.

Fight Japanese Beetles

Plant larkspur in your vegetable garden. The beetles will be attracted to the larkspur and leave the vegetables to you.

Avoid Aphids—When You Can

Tulip trees and maple trees attract aphids. Remember that when you are planting new trees. Both are beautiful trees, but maples have another drawback—you cannot plant anything under them, because of their shallow roots. If you still want them (and I don't blame you), plant them away from your flower or vegetable garden.

Found: A Use for Wild Onion

You probably have it in your lawn—so many people do. It looks like a scallion, and when you pull it up, it has a bulb at the end just like a scallion. Grind it up with some hot pepper and throw in some old onions if you have any. Add an equal amount of water and boil. Strain it through cloth and use this juice to spray your plants. It will discourage cabbage worms, caterpillars, ants and spiders.

Homemade Mosquito Repellent

Rub your skin with apple-cider vinegar before going to an area where you know mosquitoes abide. You'll drive them away. People, too, if you put too much on.

In Case You Need a Reason for Feeding Birds

One chickadee will destroy more than 138 cankerworm eggs. A quail taken in Pennsylvania had eaten over 100 potato bugs. One in Texas was found to have 127 boll weevils in its craw. A tree swallow's stomach revealed 40 chinch bugs, and the stomach of a killdeer contained 300 mosquito larvae. Now, *that's* bug control.

WILD LIFE IN YOUR GARDEN— NO ROMANCE BUT LOTS OF ACTION

Keep Raccoons out of Corn

Raccoons will eat every luscious ear of corn you grow, and if you're like I am, corn—fresh corn—is the most delicious thing you can eat. Here's my secret way to keep those eye-appealing but destructive pests out of the garden. It's so simple that it's ridiculous. Put a portable radio in a plastic bag, tune it to an all-night news station and place it in the middle of your corn garden. The bag, of course, will protect the radio from the elements. The bad news one hears constantly on the radio is enough to drive anybody away—even raccoons.

Another Way to Get Rid of Raccoons

Cayenne pepper works pretty well. Either grind hot-pepper pods or use powdered cayenne. Use ½ teaspoonful of soap powder and 2 tablespoons of water for each 2 tablespoons of pepper. Strain and spray on the plants. The soap powder helps the spray stick to the leaves.

Be Kind to Skunks

Skunks have bad scents but good sense. They destroy vast quantities of harmful insects. During some seasons they feed on nothing else. They like army worms, tobacco worms, white grubs, cutworms, potato beetles, grasshoppers, and a host of other little dastards. One time they were so helpful to the hop growers in New York State by destroying hop grubs that a law was passed, at the insistence of the hop growers, protecting skunks from being killed.

How to Keep Dogs Away from Favorite Plants

Dogs, like many adults, hate the smell of cigars and cigarettes. Put all old cigar and cigarette butts in a bowl of water. Soak strips of rag in that butt water and then tie the strips around the plants you don't want the dogs to violate.

How to Outwit Moles

When you see a mole track in your garden, make small holes along it, and sprinkle some red pepper into them.

More on Moles

I know a woman who swears by this method. She has a large dog that produces large droppings. She dropped those droppings into the mole hole. The mole or moles couldn't take it, and left—thanks to Rover.

Another Way to Fight Moles—and Gophers, Too

These sneaky little critters do such a great deal of damage that it's worth trying everything. Try either sand or fiberglass insulation, both of which you can get free by using your charm around a building site. Put the sand or the fiberglass insulation in the critters' tunnels. If it's sand, their tunnels will collapse. If it's fiberglass, it will stick in their paws. They'll cry "uncle" before you do.

How to Repel Rabbits and Deer

It's very difficult to deter these two without hurting them. Some people have had luck with wood ashes sprinkled around the plants the animals like. The only trouble with this is that the wood ashes must be replenished after watering or rain. Wood ashes, by the way, are also anathema to slugs and cutworms.

Another Bunny Baffler

Experts claim that moist bark is the secret to a better shaped apple tree and more apples. A good way to moisten the bark, and at the same time to keep rabbits from chewing on the sweet bark, is to wrap the trunk of the young tree with strips of old nylon stockings. Then pour water inside the strips. They will keep the bark moist. Repeat when dry. The nylon will also play havoc with Br'er Rabbit's munching molars, and he'll stay away from the tree.

How to Get Rid of Woodchucks

Woodchucks leave a telltale mound of earth around the entrance to their burrows, the dummies. You play it smart by pouring about 3 tablespoons of carbon disulfide on a wad of cotton and then placing the wad in the burrow. Close the burrow with dirt and you won't have any more woodchucks. You can also use 2 tablespoons of Cyanogas, placed very deep into the burrow. Be careful of Cyanogas, though; it's a deadly poison, and some states have outlawed it.

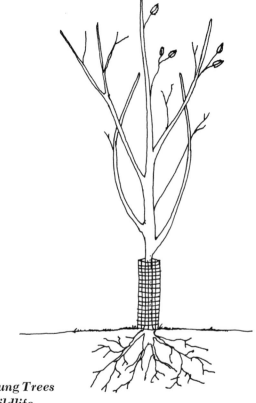

Another Way to Protect Young Trees
from Friendly Wildlife

Animals that chew, scratch or wet can harm saplings. Don't cry, complain or shoot, when all you have to do is wrap wire mesh around the trunk to protect your little sapling. Keep the mesh loose so the tree can grow. I've heard that an aluminum strip (not foil) also works, as does a coating of lard and cayenne pepper.

Oriental Secret for Happiness

      If you wish to be happy for an hour, get drunk; for three days, kill your pig and eat it; for eight days, get married. And if you wish to be happy forever, become a gardener.

When a woman wants her husband to make a garden, the first thing he'll usually dig up is a good excuse.

MICHAEL MULLALLY

Chapter Three

Flowering Secrets

HELPING NATURE PRODUCE THE ACT NOBODY'S BEEN ABLE TO TOP

EVERYTHING YOU NEED TO KNOW ABOUT ROSES— (AND SOME THINGS YOU MAY WISH YOU DIDN'T)

How to "Make" a Healthier Rosebush

Epsom salts will do it. Yep. Good old-fashioned Epsom salts. Just sprinkle about 2 ounces around each bush, and water thoroughly. Your bush will branch more often, and you'll see a fine production of healthy green leaves.

Save Your Hair for Your Roses

Human hair is a rich natural source of nitrogen. Roses love it. So will your compost heap. Charm your local barber or dog-clipping parlor into saving all clients' hair, and dig it into the soil around your plants. Experiments with over 30 varieties of roses have shown that when human hair is mixed with the soil, the roses have larger buds, deeper color and longer stems. That's as good a reason as any for splitting hairs.

How to Keep Rose Roots Cool

Roses love to have cool feet. Plant violets under your rose-bushes. That will do the trick, and very prettily, too.

How to Use a Hose Without Making Water Holes in the Ground

Here's a humdinger for watering when you want to leave the hose on the ground for a good soaking. Put the nozzle into an empty flower pot turned on its side in a saucer. The water will run through the drainage holes and flow over the saucer into the ground without making a hole, no matter how hard you have the water turned on. This simple genius of an idea is the poor man's answer to the soaker, ideal for watering plants such as roses, where you certainly don't want to make any holes or wet the roses or their foliage.

Homemade Insect Spray for Roses

I know a woman who swears by her garlic spray for getting rid of rose pests. She boils a whole bulb of garlic—cut up, of course—and when it's soft, throws it into a gallon of water. She adds 1 table-spoon of detergent, the biodegradable kind. Then she strains the mixture, puts it in her spray can, holds her nose and sprays away. She finds it perfect for use on roses.

About Cultivation and Its Pitfalls

If you don't mulch your roses, then you must cultivate the soil around them to get rid of weeds. Do this by loosening it or digging in it. Watch that you don't cultivate too deeply, or you'll cut the roots that are near the surface.

Rules About Pruning Roses

Spring's the time to prune your hybrid tea roses, by cutting them back to 8 inches above the ground. At the same time you should cut floribundas back to 12 to 15 inches. In the fall, prune everblooming climbers by removing at the base the canes that bore the summer beauties. Be sure you don't cut the new shoots, or you won't have any flowers next summer.

Want Roses That Smell?

For so long we've had beautiful new hybrid roses with one flaw—no fragrance. We were made to feel that we had to sacrifice fragrance for beauty. Not so anymore, anyway. Under a bequest made by a wonderful human being, Dr. Alexander Gamble, fragrance in roses has once again come into its own. Awards are given to roses strictly for their "delightful fragrance." Award winners include Crimson Glory, Chrysler Imperial, Sutter's Gold, Tiffany, Granada and Fragrant Cloud. There are others—you just have to nose around to find them.

What to Use in a Potpourri

Many people don't even know about the lovely old-fashioned custom of mixing dried petals of roses with spices and keeping them in a jar or bowl for their fragrance. Pity. To those of you who like to make a potpourri occasionally, may I suggest you try the old-fashioned rose geranium (*Pelargonium gravolens*)? This rose-scented beauty has as sweet a fragrance as any rose, and it lasts longer than real roses. The leaves retain their odor for many years. Of course, if you're a creature of habit, use regular rose petals. No matter which, it's still a delightful custom.

Prevent Black Spot on Rosebushes

Planting a tomato next to a rosebush will inhibit black spot. The tomato leaves contain solamine, which black spot cannot tolerate. If you don't want tomato plants upstaging your roses, set out small tomato plants, and when they get large, replace them.

Another way to get rid of black spot organically is to grind up a large bunch of tomato leaves and add 5 pints of water and 1 ounce of cornstarch. Keep the solution refrigerated. Spray on your rosebushes once a week. This mixture is good not only for black spot but for aphids, cabbage butterfly and squash borers as well.

Roses, Onions, and Black Spot

Roses grown near any member of the onion family are less likely to develop black spot than roses planted where there are no onions. Curiously enough, black spot is found only on roses that grow where the air is fairly pure. It does not occur near industrial districts heavy with fumes. Sulfur in smoke fumes from industry must do to black spot what the sulfurous oil from onions does. Maybe industrial areas should soften their terrible effect on the environment by growing lots of roses.

Another Way You Might Discourage Aphids on Roses

Some people swear that geraniums or onions planted near roses will discourage aphids. See for yourself.

Aphids Again

If you won't use chemicals to get rid of aphids, and if companion planting doesn't help much, send away for some ladybugs and/or a colony of praying mantises. They'll get rid of the aphids in a hurry.

Turning "Bad" to "Good"

Sometimes you'll find that the onions you buy in a store will have little green shoots growing out of the centers. That means they have "matured" a bit on the shelf. Don't despair. They're good for cooking and for one other thing—aphids. Just cut off the root part attached to the green sprout and plant it near your roses or wherever you have aphids.

When You Don't Want to Plant Onions to Get Rid of Aphids

If you don't like the idea of onions in the rose bed, grow allium. It's a member of the onion family, but it's the pretty one. It has a beautiful bloom in the shape of a ball. The ball itself is made up of hundreds of tiny flowers. Some alliums grow to a height of 5 feet, with blossom heads up to 8 inches in diameter. Their colors are magnificent, too. Take your pick from blue, purple, white, greenish-white, yellow, rose and dark red. Alliums are winter-hardy and require the same care as onions. Plant the bulbs in the spring at a depth of four times the diameter of the bulb, but never deeper than 4 inches.

Another Safeguard for Roses

If you plant parsley as an edging around your roses, you'll help reduce attacks of aphids.

Mulching with Grass

Some people swear by it. Others claim that the many fungi found in grass these days will produce fungus disease on the plants that are mulched with it. To play it safe, don't mulch your roses with grass clippings. Use peat moss instead, but don't allow it to cake on the surface or it will prevent water from getting to the roots.

Try This Fantastic Rose

If you can find it, get the New Dawn climbing rose. It produces loads of single pink roses that send me into an ecstasy every time I look at them.

How to Take a Super Rose Picture Right on the Bush

Use an empty picture frame to frame the rose or roses the way you want them. Then shoot. You can get some really unique shots this way. The frame will stand by itself on the bush, so you don't need anyone to mastermind your masterpiece.

How to Handle Thorny Rose Stems

Simply clamp a clothespin (the spring type) over the stem and cut away.

How to Tell Whether a Rose Will Last in Water

Simply pinch the bud. It should be firm and full. If it is soft, the flower will open and die quickly. When a rose is partially open and the petals are limp, the rose will not last in water. Roses must be firm and resilient to last in an arrangement.

How to Make Candied Rose Petals

These are really delightful, delicious and decorative things to use as a garnish for a fruit cup, as a decoration on cakes, as a border for a dessert, or on a cake plate. Actually, there are many uses for these lovely-to-look-at candied rose petals. They're so easy to make, too. All you do is beat one egg white in a small bowl. Leave it while you sprinkle a layer of sugar on a plate. Now dip rose petals, and leaves, too, first in the egg white and then in the sugar. Make sure both sides are coated. Dry on a rack. If you're not going to use them right away, put them on wax paper and separate the layers with paper toweling.

Rose Hips—Better Than Oranges

Would you believe that rose hips, those pods that appear on your bush after the petals drop, are richer than oranges in vitamin C? Some rose hips, especially those from *Rosa rugosa*, are 60 times richer in vitamin C than oranges. Rose hips are really the fruit of the rose, and their flavor when ripe is both fruity and spicy. You can eat them right off the bush, but you'll also find a great many fun recipes calling for them.

More About Rose Hips

If you're going to collect rose hips from wild roses (a great way to spend a day in the country), be sure to wear gloves. Rose hips are very astringent and can make your fingers insensitive to touch for several days.

Sherbet from Your Roses

Be the first on your block to serve rose sherbet. I'm not fooling. It's made from rose petals, and it's delish.

1 pint of rose petals (try the fragrant ones)
2¼ cups of granulated sugar
Juice of 6 fresh oranges, strained

Wash petals and gradually add ¼ cup of the sugar. Pound into a paste. Dissolve the remaining sugar in 4 cups of boiling water. Stir in the rose paste. Boil mixture for 10 minutes *without stirring*. (Not even one stir.) Let cool. Add orange juice. Freeze. When you serve it, decorate it with fresh rose petals. It's a delight.

Rose Water for Your Hair

Here's a delightful old-fashioned treatment for hair that's especially good as a rinse for oily hair. Gather rose petals early in the morning, put them in an enameled pot, barely cover them with water, and slowly bring the mixture to a boil. Simmer for two to four minutes and strain. It's not only good as a rinse for hair, but it's very delightful for the face, too. Rose water, by the way, is used in many countries as a flavoring for food. In India it's used to flavor sherbet, ice cream and cakes. The Arabs use it as a glaze when roasting fowl. Taste it and you'll get ideas of your own.

How to Be an Instant Garden Expert

Roses have been cultivated for thousands of years. The Chinese were growing them almost 3,000 years before Christ, during the Shen Nung dynasty. And we have proof from paintings found on the island of Crete that roses were cultivated there more than 4,000 years ago. I wonder how many aphids we've had in 4,000 years.

FROM THE NEVER-FORGET-IT DEPARTMENT

Prevent Mildew on Dahlias

Dahlias, along with lilac and stock, are very susceptible to mildew, especially when the evenings are cool and the mornings dew-heavy. Provide air circulation around the dahlias by gently pulling off the bottom row of leaves. If you have about 8 to 12 inches of clear space under the plant, you'll help prevent the problem.

Keep Dahlias Watered

Dahlias are guzzlers. They need lots of water, not so much to survive as to produce their sensational flowers. Just a temporary lack of water can set plants back as much as three weeks, or even permanently.

How to Get More Clematis Blooms

Pruning is the secret. You do it early in the season, when the new growth is 2 to 2½ feet high. Pinch off not quite half of the growing tips on the lengthening vines. This will cause a second crop of flowers to appear three or four weeks after the first bloom. If you've never grown clematis, you should know that you must water the plants at ground level only, avoiding the flowers and foliage.

How to Get More Flowers from Your Geraniums

Keep your geraniums pot-bound. In other words, don't change pots until you see roots coming out of the bottom of the pot. When you are using geraniums in big tubs for summer color, plant pot and all in the tub to get a lot of color fast.

Prevent Spindly Begonias

When wax begonia plants become spindly and weak, it's because you're either overwatering them or not pinching them back regularly. You can cut them drastically. Shear them straight across, an inch above the soil. With a little love and care they'll come back beautifully. Feed them with a 7-6-19 fertilizer. That's one low in nitrogen (7) and phosphorus (6), and high in potash (19). A fertilizer within this range will help your begonia produce more flowers.

How to Stop Buds from Blooming Too Soon

There's always a time when you wish the flowers you're planning to use in arrangements would not bloom too soon. Well, now you don't have to wish. Just try my secret for holding back the bloom by putting your flowers in the refrigerator. First, cover each bud with tissue paper, then pack each flower, stem and all, in its own plastic bag and stick all the bags in the refrigerator. The day before you're planning to use them, cut off a tiny bit of stem and stand the flowers in tepid water in a cool place. Daffodils, peonies and roses are among those that work quite well with this method.

No-Cost Plant Ties

Old nylon stockings are fit to be tied. Cut them up in strips for tying plants to stakes. You can use nylon strips to tie everything from alliums to zinnias. You can even dye them green to blend in with your garden. In any event, they are as gentle to your plants as they are to your legs.

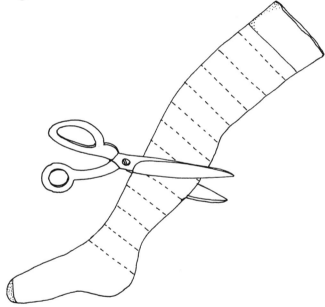

Increase Your Garden Knowledge

Did you know that in Victorian times foxglove was brewed and taken by the elderly for heart murmurs? That catnip tea was prescribed for colds?

MORE FERTILIZING SECRETS

The Stuff Award-Winning Plants Are Made Of

How would you like to turn ordinary geraniums into plants with luxuriant deep green growth and giant flower heads of intensified color? Who wouldn't? There is a secret way to do this. Few growers in America know about it, although it's popular in England. It just might be the reason the English have such remarkable flowers. You've simply got to try it, because the results are so spectacular they are unbelievable. You need two things: Epsom salts and saltpeter. To get bigger, greener leaves—almost twice their normal size—spray the leaves every 10 to 14 days with a handful (2 ounces) of Epsom salts mixed with 2 gallons of water. It doesn't matter if some of the solution goes into the soil, but try to aim for the leaves, because the Epsom salts are strictly for foliar feeding.

To get the most fabulous blooms, so rich in color they almost glow in the dark, use a level teaspoon of saltpeter to a gallon of water and pour enough of this mixture on the soil to thoroughly moisten it. On the soil, not on the leaves. This fantastic secret is marvelous not only for geraniums but for other flowers, too. Try it outdoors on roses. Wow! Experiment—you may just end up with a giant of a garden, inside and out. Go slowly at first, one plant at a time.

Fish Heads for Fertilizer

Charm the man who sells you your fish into giving you some fish heads—free, of course. Bury them near roses or other favorite plants. They decompose quite quickly and will provide your soil with both nitrogen and phosphorus. Bury them deeply, or a dog will get them. The Indians were great fish users. They buried an entire fish for every stalk of corn they planted.

How to Make a Home Any Worm Would Love
Worms do so much for your soil that you must encourage them to live in your garden. One way is to leave all the leaves that fall into your garden beds just where they fall. Then cover them with a thin blanket of salt hay—just enough to keep them from blowing away. The leaves retain moisture and attract earthworms. The worms, in turn, help break down the leaves into a rich compost, which can then be turned into your soil in the spring.

Another Fertilizer You Can Make Yourself
Save all your eggshells. When you have a sufficient number, put them into the blender and grind them to a coarse powder. Mix with water and feed to your plants.

ATTRACTING FRIENDS THAT FLY

Want More Butterflies in Your Garden?
Grow the butterfly bush—buddleia. It's also known as summer lilac, and it comes in a variety of marvelous colors. When it's not in flower, it resembles a small-leaf weeping willow. When it is in bloom, it's like a waterfall of color. The butterflies aren't the only creatures that will love your buddleia. You will, too.

Attract the Sparrows to Your Garden
Our native sparrows are probably the greatest weed-seed eaters of all birds. As a group they undoubtedly eat more seed than all

other birds combined. One man estimated that on an acre of land on a Maryland farm, the 500 birds found there destroyed more than 40,000 weed seeds at one meal alone!

How to Make Birds Come Closer to Your Window

Here's a Sneaky-Pete idea that really works. Put your bird feeder on a clothesline or a trolley with a wire extending from a near-by tree to your windowsill. Start with the bird feeder nearer the tree.

After the birds get used to it, move it a few feet closer to the house each day. In a short time, they'll be accustomed to the closeness. If the operation is a gradual one, you'll be able to see them eyeball-to-eyeball. A bird's-eye view, so to speak.

How to Be an Instant Garden Expert

Did you know that a bee flies 35,500 miles in order to gather enough nectar for one pound of honey? That's more than once around the world. Who figured that out—and how—I can't tell you.

GOOD FOR WHAT'S BUGGING YOU

How to Remain Sane While Reading Garden-Chemical Labels

It seems to me that all manufacturers of sprays, liquid fertilizers and the like think all gardeners have tremendous acreage. The poor soul who has only a sliver of ground and needs only a cupful of spray is hard put to get it when the label gives dilution directions for gallons. Here's a conversion table you ought to frame:

DILUTION REQUIRED	PER GALLON OF WATER	PER QUART OF WATER
1 part to 1000 parts	3/4 teaspoon	3/16 teaspoon
1 part to 750 parts	1 teaspoon	1/4 teaspoon
1 part to 555 parts	1/2 tablespoon	3/8 teaspoon
1 part to 250 parts	1 tablespoon	3/4 teaspoon
1 part to 200 parts	1 1/4 tablespoons	15/16 teaspoon
1 part to 150 parts	1 2/3 tablespoons	1 1/4 teaspoons
1 part to 100 parts (1%)	2 1/2 tablespoons	1 7/8 teaspoons
1 part to 50 parts (2%)	5 tablespoons	3 3/4 teaspoons
1 part to 33 parts (3%)	7 1/2 tablespoons	5 5/8 teaspoons
1 part to 25 parts (4%)	10 tablespoons	7 1/2 teaspoons
1 part to 20 parts (5%)	12 tablespoons	9 teaspoons
1 part to 15 parts (7 1/2%)	18 tablespoons	13 1/2 teaspoons
1 part to 10 parts (10%)	25 1/2 tablespoons	19 1/8 teaspoons
1 part to 5 parts (20%)	51 1/5 tablespoons	38 2/5 teaspoons

MEASUREMENT EQUIVALENTS BY VOLUME

1 gallon = 4 quarts = 8 pints = 16 cups
1 quart = 2 pints = 4 cups = 64 tablespoons
1 pint = 2 cups = 32 tablespoons
1 cup = 16 tablespoons = 48 teaspoons
1 tablespoon = 3 teaspoons

How to Use an Insecticide on Plants with Waxy Leaves

Waxy leaves are difficult to spray because the insecticide simply rolls off. My secret for avoiding this is to simply add one-half teaspoonful of a mild dishwashing detergent to each gallon of spray. The detergent not only will improve the wetting power of your mixture, but will also reduce any residue that may look unpleasant on the leaves.

How to Kill 'Em with Garlic

The ancients knew about garlic and its marvelous ability to control mosquito larvae, aphids, and the like. Today's scientists seem to be just getting around to accepting the fact that garlic does more than make food taste superb. They admit that garlic's active component is allyl sulfide, which is found in the bulbs of all members of the onion family.

How to Make a Garlic Insecticide

Here's the method used by many organic gardeners. Chop 3 ounces of garlic bulbs (the homegrown ones are best) and soak in 2 teaspoonfuls of mineral oil for 24 hours. Put ¼ ounce of dishwashing liquid into a pint of water and add it slowly to the garlic mixture. Mix well. Strain it through cheesecloth and store it in a glass or china container. Never use metal. When ready to spray, dilute it—try one part to twenty parts of water.

More on How to Kill 'Em with Garlic

Here's another reliable garlic spray. Put three cloves of garlic, one medium-sized chopped onion and two cups of water into the blender and blend for about a minute. Next pour the mixture into a saucepan, add two teaspoons of hot red-pepper sauce and steep this witch's brew for 24 hours. Strain through cheesecloth or a nylon stocking, and you've got a concentrate that's strong enough to kill.

Before you use it in your spray, dilute with five cups of water. This spray not only will help get rid of aphids, but will keep our furry friends away, too. Rabbits and woodchucks especially don't like that hot red-pepper sauce. Don't throw away the solid part you strained out—bury it, cheesecloth and all, in the area where you have the greatest problem.

Another Idea

If garlic is too strong for your garden's nose, make your insecticide out of scallions. Let the scallions soak in water overnight, and the next day spray the solution on your roses and any other plants attacked by aphids. It really works.

How to Kill 'Em with Pepper

Pepper is pretty effective against cucumber beetles and corn borers, and a pepper spray is easy to brew. Simply combine 3 tablespoons of ground pepper with 3 cups of boiling water. When cool, add 2 tablespoons of soap powder; shake, pour into a spray can, and "bombs away!" The soap powder will help the spray stick to the foliage.

What to Do for Ants Everywhere Except in Pants

Ants won't hurt your plants, but somehow they attract aphids, and aphids hurt. Try bone meal sprinkled on soil or lawn. Powdered charcoal sprinkled around the plants might help, too. Ants in the house can be deterred if you watch where they make their entrance. Then squeeze some lemon juice around it.

How to Get Rid of Aphids on Nasturtiums

Nasturtiums are often used to lure insects away from other plants. They certainly lure all the aphids onto their own leaves. When that condition exists, it's because of little or no lime in the soil. Try dusting your plants with lime (limestone, not the fruit), and the aphids will disappear.

How to Get Rid of Whitefly—Maybe

These little dastards are the bane of any gardener's life. They are one of the most, if not *the* most, difficult insects to control. There is nothing more aggravating than to touch a leaf of a cucumber, tomato, melon or houseplant and to have these fly out from under it in a cloud—like flying dandruff.

The female of this despicable species lays about 150 eggs, which hatch in about 10 days. There haven't been many chemicals that have been able to control whitefly, except those that are very toxic to human beings. You've got to use something that will coat the eggs with a film, to prevent hatching. Ask your garden supplier for a "spray oil" which can coat the eggs. When you use it, be sure you thoroughly cover the plant so that you don't miss any eggs. New chemicals are coming out all the time, and perhaps there will be a new one for whitefly by the time this is printed.

Hope for Biological Control of Whitefly

In 1973 some professional growers found an effective bio-logical control for this pest, in the form of a small parasite known as *Encarsia formosa*. It's about 1/40 inch long. Almost all of them are females which can reproduce without mating. They lay eggs in each whitefly, causing it to die and turn black, so it looks like a speck of pepper. But even with this remarkable helper, you cannot always get 100 percent whitefly control.

What to Do About Beetles When All Else Fails

Nothing seems to stop Japanese beetles when there's a juicy rosebush to nibble on. Actually, they eat over 200 kinds of plants, but roses are by far their favorite. Sometimes they ignore the poisonous sprays and eat on to oblivion. If you don't want to use chemical sprays, and companion plants known to deter beetles are not deterring, cover your rosebush with a mesh netting or cheesecloth.

Another Slug Remover

This time, eggshells. Good, reliable eggshells. They get rid of ants; they make a good fertilizer; and now we find they can be crushed and sprinkled along the edge of the garden bed where the slugs are. The shells will stick to them, and they'll scatter.

More on Flowers That Discourage Insects

Some flowers planted near vegetable gardens can do a lot more than look pretty. Cosmos, asters, chrysanthemums, pyrethrum (or painted daisies)—all have strong aromas which can help foil a number of pests. Nasturtiums and marigolds benefit both flower and vegetable gardens, and I hear that nasturtiums are particularly good around fruit trees. Nasturtiums also keep aphids, squash bugs and striped pumpkin beetles from devastating your vegetables.

Tansy does a very good job of discouraging ants. Planted by the door, it helps keep both ants and flies out of the house. What's more, Japanese beetles don't go near berries or cane fruits when tansy is planted nearby.

Become an Instant Garden Expert

Did you know that many insect-killing and -repelling ingredients are made from pyrethrum, which is that lovely painted daisy you may be growing in your garden? It takes 80 pounds of dried painted daisies to make one pound of insecticide compound.

Choose the Right Nasturtium

As I have said, the pungent odor of nasturtium is absolutely repulsive to aphids and whiteflies. Also, the roots of the plant give off a substance that will deter root lice. However, the new-fangled nasturtiums don't seem to have the fragrance that displeases these pests. When you buy seed, be sure the description in the seed catalog mentions fragrance. That's the one to buy. Incidentally, unripe nasturtium seeds can be used for pickles.

OUTWITTING THE WILDLIFE

How to Get Rid of Rabbits and Deer—Painlessly

Sprinkle some dried blood on the plants you don't want deer or rabbits to chew on. Not only will blood deter the animals, but it will give the plants' foliage a rich, lush look and make the flowers larger than usual. You can purchase dried blood in bags at your local garden shop.

How to Get Rid of Moles

You'll find the active mole tunnel if you first flatten all of them. The one that opens up the next day is your target. Set a mouse trap in the tunnel at a right angle and cover it with a basket or box in order to keep out light. If you don't want to kill the mole, red pepper will send it off to bother someone else.

Another Way to Foil Moles (and Gophers)

Castor oil. It drives away humans, so why not moles and gophers? Several people I know swear by this method. Put 2 ounces of castor oil and 1 ounce of liquid detergent into a bowl and whip until thick as shaving cream. Add water equal to the volume of the mixture and whip again. Fill your sprinkling can with warm water, add about 2 tablespoons of the castor-oil goody, stir well and sprinkle over the areas of heaviest infestation. If you do it after a good watering of the soil or a good rain, your castor-oil delight will penetrate better.

And Still Another Way to Get Rid of Moles

Since castor oil is made from the castor bean plant, moles obviously don't like the plant, either. Plant one or two castor bean plants about 25 to 30 feet apart around the area of mole infestation. They grow very, very high (some as high as seven feet), with lots of branches, which are covered with large tropical leaves. They grow in a hurry, too. The plants and seeds are poisonous, and the moles stay away from them.

How to Be an Instant Garden Expert

Did you know a mole weighing 3 ounces can eat 2 ounces of food daily? Their favorite food is worms. One 50-gram mole can eat

65 grams of worms in a 24-hour period. (Who cares, except maybe another mole—or a worm.)

How to Repel Flies and Ants

You can do it with tansy—an old-fashioned herb that is not only attractive but most useful. Planted by the kitchen door, it will help keep away flies and ants. They evidently don't like its spicy odor. Tansy, unfortunately, is not too well known in this country these days. Yet in Colonial times its leaves were used to make a tea that was used as a remedy for worms in children, hysteria, gout, fevers, and even measles. The dried tansy leaves, sprinkled on food, served as a substitute for pepper, nutmeg and cinnamon.

Since we're all on a nostalgia kick, it would be worthwhile to revive tansy and make it a household word—or at least a familiar name in the garden. It's a fast-spreading plant and could almost be called a shrub, as it grows 4 to 5 feet high. It has beautiful leaves resembling those of fern, and the flowers look like tiny yellow buttons. Tansy *(Tanacetum vulgare)* belongs to the aster family. It grows best in full sun and is really a lovely plant to have in your garden. Its leaves can be used in Christmas wreaths, and they are also delightfully spicy and good to use when storing woolens and furs. Then, too, you can put the leaves in a bowl to counteract stale odors in a room. You can't buy tansy seed everywhere, but here are a few sources:

Nichols Garden Nursery
   1190 North Pacific Hwy., Albany, Oregon 97321
Green Herb Gardens
   Greene, Rhode Island 02827
Well-Sweep Farm
   451 Mt. Bethel Road, Port Murray, New Jersey 07865

How to Keep Tansy from Taking Over Your Garden

Plant it in a plastic bag and then plant the bag in the ground. The roots will become "bag bound," and the growth will be more compact and less able to wander around.

> *Don't plant more garden than your wife can take care of.*
>
> HENRI NIER

Chapter Four

Cutting Secrets

THE KINDEST CUT(S) OF ALL

**PROLONGING NATURE'S
GREATEST ACT**

The Best Time to Cut Flowers

Late in the day. The very last hours of daylight are really the best time for cutting. Plants build up a food supply throughout the sunny hours, and because they do they will last longer on a full stomach than on an empty one. The second-best time to cut is very early in the morning, before the sun is high—before the dew has dried on the petals and before the bees and the butterflies have done their thing. Unpollinated cut flowers last longer in water.

How to Make Cut Flowers Last

To get flowers to last a decent length of time, it is necessary to keep air out of their stems. Once they are cut, the air rushes in, and that's the beginning of the flower's end. The trick, therefore, is to prevent the air from going up into the stem. The way to do it is to take a pot of very hot water and a pot of cold water into the garden with you while you are cutting. Plunge the cut stem into that hot water to seal it. Then drop the entire stem into the pail of cold water. If carrying two pails of water is not your bag, take a pail of cold water into the garden and put the flowers in it as you cut them. Then, when you're arranging them in the house, plunge the cut ends into hot water for a few seconds. Make sure the steam does not touch the blossoms; it will blacken them.

Another Way to Make Flowers Last Longer

Some flower stems contain a milky juice, and once that juice hits the air after the stems are cut, the flowers begin to droop. To prevent this, sear the stem immediately after cutting. A cigarette lighter is the handiest tool for this, but a match or even a candle will do. (I'll admit you'll look pretty silly holding a lit candle in broad daylight.) Some of the plants that need this kind of hot foot are poinsettia, mignonette, heliotrope, hollyhock, morning glory, milkweed, pokeweed and ferns.

Keep Your Cut Flowers Cool

Help make your flower arrangements last longer by placing them in a cool spot in the evening. Even placing them on the floor before you go to bed could add days to their life. Just remember—heat rises, so cool it, baby.

Aspirin and Pennies Are Not for Cut Flowers

The old wives' tale of putting an aspirin or a penny in a vase of freshly cut flowers to make them last longer is just that—an old wives' tale. Neither will do a bit of good.

How to Tell Whether Your Water Is Right for
Your Cut Flowers

I'll bet you've never heard of this—but just as you can test your soil for its acid and alkaline content, so too can you test the water you put your cut flowers in. They live best in water that has a pH of 4. Buy some litmus paper at the drugstore to test your water. If the pH is too high, just add 3 heaping teaspoons of sugar and 2 tablespoons of distilled white vinegar to each quart of water. This formula is the proper one to lower a pH from 7 to 4, but you can work out your own formula from that, depending on the pH of your water.

The Right Room Temperature for Cut Flowers

The *Journal of the Royal Horticultural Society* in England recently reported a test that was made to determine how long cut flowers will last indoors. Although some flowers last longer than others, it was determined that cut flowers will often last three weeks at a temperature of 50°, five to six days at a temperature of 60° to 65°, and only two to three days when kept at a temperature of 70°. Furthermore, a cool room is a better holding spot for cut flowers than a cold refrigerator.

Where to Cut the Rose

Just remember: the more you cut, the more you get, if you cut at the right spot. Cut just above a leaf with five leaflets, not one with three leaflets. Leave at least two sets of five-leaflet leaves on the stems, if possible.

How to Extend the Life of Your Cut Roses

Take a tip from the commercial growers. Here's how they do it. They call it "hardening," and it can extend the life of a cut rose from 3 days to 8 days in most cases. Add a preservative to some water. Stand your roses in the water in the coolest spot in your house for 24 hours.

How to Handle Cut Flowers After You've
Put Them in Water

Cut flowers, like most houseplants, like a humid atmosphere. After you've perfected your arrangement, give it a spray with a fine mist of cold water. Spray not only into the flowers and leaves, but also into the air above the arrangement. This will increase the humidity in the room and will also prevent undue loss of moisture from flowers and leaves.

How to Care for Cut Roses

The best time to cut roses is around dusk or shortly before. Remember to cut above a leaf that has five leaflets—not one with three leaflets. Place the roses in deep cold water, foliage and all, right up to but not including the bloom. Keep them there for several hours or overnight. If the roses on the bush look as if they will come into bloom before they are needed, cut them as described above and then strip the lower leaves so that no leaves will be in the water. Put the roses, container and all, into a clear plastic cleaner's bag. Place a stick in the middle of the roses, long enough to reach above the tallest bloom, so there will be no pressure from the plastic cover on your flowers. Tie the plastic bag at the top and put the whole thing in the coolest spot you have. Check often to see that no moisture has formed on roses that have already opened, since the moisture will discolor the blooms. If flowers seem unusually moist, turn the plastic bag inside out so that the dry side is on the inside, next to the roses.

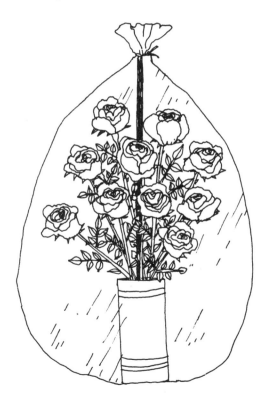

How to Prevent Tulips from Drooping

Wrap tulips in wet newspaper and put them, newspaper and all, into a very tall container of cold water. The container should be as tall as the flower heads. (A big pail would be perfect.) Leave

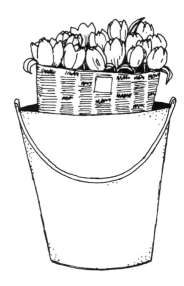

them in the container overnight. If they droop after a few days, rewrap them in another wet newspaper. Incidentally, tulips always turn their faces toward the light after they have been cut. Keep this in mind when you're deciding where to put them in your arrangement.

How to Manipulate Tulip Stems Your Way

When you want tulip stems with a curve, simply hang them over the side of the container while they are soaking.

How to Make Tulip Leaves More Graceful

Tulip leaves are stubborn. Don't let them intimidate you when arranging. Tape a piece of fine wire to the back of the leaf. Then you can make it bend in any direction you desire.

How to Keep Cut Rhododendron Longer

Dunk both flowers and stems in cold water immediately after cutting and keep them there from one to two hours, or until the flowers are crisp like lettuce. Then split the stems at the base so that water can be absorbed more easily.

How to Treat Zinnias After Cutting

Whenever possible, cut zinnias when their moisture content is high—after a rain or a good soil soaking. Remove lower leaves and any others you won't need for your arrangement. Removing their leaves seems to prolong their life. As soon as you do that, put them into cold water.

How to Make Cut Violets Last Longer

Pick them when the flowers are fully opened, because the buds won't open after they are cut. Immediately dunk the entire bunch of violets into cold water for an hour. They'll float to the top, but push them back gently so that all the flowers end up soaking wet. When they are crisp like fresh lettuce, shake them free of excess water and put them in your arrangements.

How to Keep Orchids Longer

When the only cool spot you have to hold orchids is your refrigerator, wrap them in wax paper or a plastic bag to prevent them from drying out. Try not to get the petals wet. When you're using orchids in arrangements, keep the flowers from becoming waterlogged by taking the stems out of water each day for one-half to three-quarters of an hour. Then put them back in fresh water.

How to Help Marigolds Last After They Are Cut

You won't believe it, but the secret is to keep them out of water after they are cut. Keep them out for about 30 minutes. A small loss of water at this time keeps them from getting any older. Zinc sulfate, which you can buy at any drugstore, helps keep the marigolds' stems from decaying in water. Use one teaspoonful of the crystals to each quart of water. Always remember to cut marigolds when the petals are reflexed and the centers tight.

How to Help Pansies Stay Around Longer

Pull the blossoms instead of cutting them. Pull gently; they'll come away from the plant quite easily and won't disturb the roots.

How to Make Hydrangea Last Longer When Cut

Hold the stems in 2 to 3 inches of boiling vinegar for about 30 seconds. You can also submerge the flower heads in cold water until the petals are crisp.

How to Prolong the Life of Cut Gardenias

Sprinkle the gardenias, both flower and foliage, with a fine mist of cold water; or, easier still, submerge the entire flower in cold water until the petals are firm. Each night, turn the flowers face down in the water to prolong their life. Remember, try not to touch the flowers—they quickly turn brown when you do.

Cut Dahlias Like the Pros

This secret came from a very well known flower-show judge who should know what she is talking about. Soak the soil around the plants 6 or 8 hours before cutting. Evening is the best time to cut dahlias. Carry a pail of water with you, preferably warm water, and a sharp, sharp knife. Cut the stems on an angle and immediately dunk them into the water to stop the air from entering the stem shafts. Leave them in the pail for several hours or overnight in a dark, draftless area. You'll be amazed by what a little loving care can do to a dahlia.

Another Way to Help Dahlias Last Longer

Put a pinch of saltpeter in the dahlias' water. If you're cutting dahlias for exhibition, remove any foliage that might remain in the water and place stems immediately in cold water for a couple of hours. Then dip bundles of the dahlia stems in a pan of very hot water for a few seconds. (The heat destroys air pockets and makes it easier for water intake.) Finally, place stems in a deep vase of cold water, put the vase in a cool spot, and allow the dahlias to luxuriate there overnight.

How to Keep Chrysanthemums Longer in Water

Here's a great secret. Add 3 to 4 level tablespoons of sugar to each quart of cold water you keep your annual mums in. For perennial mums, split their woody stems anywhere from 2 to 5 inches and put the stems in hot water (100°F) to which you have added 4 level tablespoons of sugar per quart.

How to Prolong the Life of Bittersweet

Bittersweet berries are so beautiful in autumn, and although they last quite a long time, it isn't long enough. With this secret you can make them last almost indefinitely. Cut the branches as soon as the berries are fully developed. Spray with a shellac or plastic spray, hang upside down to dry, and then enjoy.

Make Decorative Leaves Last Longer

Calla lily, Japanese maple, hosta, ivy and begonia leaves will remain perky for days if you dunk them—really submerge them—in water for about 12 hours. Also, prick the stems of calla lily leaves with a needle.

The Right Time to Cut Gladiolus

For the prettiest effect, cut them when the second blossom is about to open.

Prevent Freshly Cut Flowers from Drooping

Flowers that have a milky or sticky juice in their stems need special treatment after cutting. This would include oriental poppies, poinsettias, and of course dahlias. Some people swear by this treatment. Put the flower stems in hot water and leave them there until the water cools. Later, if stems have to be shortened for your arrangement, char the ends with a cigarette lighter, gas flame or candle. You might try this hot-water treatment on any flower that wilts easily. Some people use it with good results on roses, penstemon, hardy asters, butterfly weed and sunflowers. Experiment yourself—with one flower at first.

How to Be an Instant Garden Expert

Did you ever hear of Joel Poinsett? He was our minister to Mexico in the early 1800s. It was he who developed the poinsettia from a Mexican plant. He cultivated it in his Charleston, South Carolina, garden and named it after himself. He deserved it. Poinsettia's botanical name is *Euphorbia pulcherrima,* meaning, I'm told, "most beautiful." That it is.

New Idea (to Some) for a Salad

Did you know that freshly cut nasturtium leaves are absolutely marvelous in a salad? They are.

Flowers That Do Better Without Water
After Cutting

Most flowers need water immediately after cutting. However, gladiolus and marigolds do better if they are left out of water for half an hour after they are cut.

Secret Way to Keep Rosebuds for Four Days

Surprise, shock and delight your friends. Send them roses through the mail. Here's my secret way to keep rosebuds cut on Monday unopened until Thursday: cut the roses in bud and slit the stems 1 inch. Put the stems in warm water for 20 minutes, then add cold water and ice cubes until everything but the buds is covered with water. Leave the stems in the ice water for 10 minutes. Now put each stem into an orchid tube (that's the little tube available at florists' that has a rubber stopper with a self-sealing hole). Fill the little tube with equal parts of ice water and 7-Up. Cover the bud with tissue paper, put it in a plastic bag and hold it in place with a twist-'em. Put the entire rose in wet newspaper and wrap it securely in aluminum foil so the package is leakproof. A little complicated, but worth the work.

How to Keep Lilies-of-the-Valley Fresh
After They Are Cut

There may be a time when your lilies-of-the-valley are ready for picking and you're not ready for them. When that happens, pick them anyway, and put their stems in cold water for 8 hours or longer. Then tie the stems together and hang them upside down in a cool spot for from 3 to 6 hours before using them.

What to Do When Hyacinths Wilt Before They Are Supposed To

Dip the ends of their stems in boiling water for no longer than 3 minutes. Then immediately put them in cold water.

SOMETIMES IT'S FUN TO FOOL MOTHER NATURE

How to Make a Night Lily Out of a Day Lily

They aren't called day lilies for nothing. They bloom only in the daytime, but you can fool them. If you want them gloriously in bloom for a dinner party or any nighttime affair, go out early in the morning on the day of your party and cut those that are going to open that day. Put them in plastic bags with tissue between the unopened blossoms. Put the bags in the refrigerator until late afternoon. Then set the stems in warm water for 15 minutes. Place them in a vase and they'll stay out later than you will.

"Paint" Your Own Flowers

You won't improve on Nature, but you can "paint" your flowers for special holidays by using ordinary food coloring. Start with white flowers such as carnations. They're the easiest. You simply put the color you want in a glass or jar, add some hot water and put the stems in. Carnations will take dye perfectly. White roses do too, but experiment. You'll find you can have orange flowers for Halloween, green for St. Patrick's Day, even red for Valentine's Day (if you can't find any red flowers already "dyed" the real thing by Mother Nature). Kids especially love to dye flowers. They and you will find that some blossoms color all over, while others show the color only in their veins for an interesting effect.

How to Make Color for Dipping Calla Lilies

Use show-card tempera, which you can get at any art store. Mix 1 tablespoon of it with 1 to 2 quarts of warm water, until you get the color you want. When the solution has cooled, dip the calla lilies into it. Ink can be used, too. Mix 1 ounce of ink and 1 heaping tablespoon of powdered alum to each pint of water, preferably rainwater.

TIPS ON FLOWER ARRANGING

For Flower Arranging—the Indispensable

No flower arranger should be without it. I'm talking about the most important item for flower arranging next to flowers. That, my friend, is Oasis, a block of porous material which is feather light when dry and very heavy when soaked in water. You stick your flower stems into it. It can hold them upright or at any angle you want. Oasis is more than marvelous, and you can buy it at any florist, nursery, or plant department. Eventually, it gets so full of holes you can't use it as a block. Then crumble it and use it for stuffing a tall vase. Even "dead" it will hold flowers upright.

How to Water Your Flower Arrangement
Without Ruining It

You can often ruin an arrangement when you try to water it. Here's how to avoid disturbing the flowers. Use an oven baster to change the water. Just draw off the old water and replace it with fresh. My oven baster works better at this than it does with a roast in the oven.

How to Take Your Flower Arrangement
for a Drive

How many times have you had a flower arrangement to transport to a flower show or to a friend in the hospital and nobody around to hold it upright while you drove? Even if you've never had the problem, you might someday. I have it constantly, and for some reason there's never anyone around when an arrangement needs to be transported. At any rate, by trial and error I've found that placing the arrangement in a box that's already in the car and then placing bricks or big stones against the box to steady it seems to solve the problem.

What to Do When Some Flower Stems Curl in Your Arrangements

Often daffodil or narcissus stems curl when they are in water. If that messes up your arrangement, simply fasten a piece of tape around the stems before you put them on the pin holder.

Curve Your Snapdragons

Spiky flowers such as snapdragon, lupine and stock grow beautifully straight, but some arrangements cry out for a curve here and there. You can put a curve in these flowers by putting them in a pail of water and allowing their ends to hang over like (for lack of a better description) a drunk on a boat in a rough sea suffering visibly from mal de mer.

How to Prevent Violet Petals from Dropping

Often an African violet—or a garden-variety violet—adds just the perfect touch to a bouquet. The trouble is the petals are so fragile they either shatter or drop. You can prevent that with a mixture of egg white and water in equal amounts. Mix the egg white by stirring, not beating. Turn the flowers face down on waxed paper or aluminum foil and carefully brush, with a Q-tip or a clean nail-polish brush, the back of each petal where it touches the calyx.

Unique Flower Holders

Save your old perfume bottles and use them as flower holders when you're giving a dinner party. Individual bouquets at everyone's plate will be the talk (and hit) of the evening—next to your food, of course.

Keep Ivy Water Sweet

If you keep a permanent arrangement of ivy in water, wash a few pieces of charcoal and throw them into the ivy water. That'll do it, as long as you change the water when it becomes cloudy.

What to Do with Artichokes When You Don't Want to Eat Them

Artichokes make gorgeous flowers in dried arrangements. Not just beautiful—gorgeous. There's nothing special you have to do to dry one, either. Just let it hang around until it is dry. Bend each leaf until it resembles a petal. If the artichoke leaves are too stiff and straight, make them pliable by holding them over steam from a teakettle. You can then bend them in any creative way you fancy. Let the artichoke dry in its new shape before you put it in your flower arrangement. Some people like to spray them a dull gold and use them in Christmas wreaths.

Make the Biggest Rose in the World

If you fold back the leaves of a red cabbage, you can, with a little creativity, transform that cabbage into a beautiful red rose. Try it. If you fail, you can eat it.

An Unusual Table Decoration

Want a conversation grabber next time you have guests? This is certainly it. Use a bromeliad, and if you don't have one, buy one. A bromeliad is any plant belonging to the pineapple family, and if you've never seen or even heard of them you've got a pleasant surprise ahead of you. Some typical ones are aechmea, guzmania and vriesia. At any rate, get yourself one of them. It will have wide-spreading leaves and a little "cup" in the middle of the leaves. The plant grows in the jungle, and that little cup catches and holds the rainwater necessary for its survival. Use that cup as a vase for cut flowers. Set the entire plant in the center of your table and you'll have a glorious table decoration as well as a conversation piece.

How to Handle Flowers with Thin Stems

Flowers such as violets have very thin stems and are not good in arrangements. But don't let that stop you. Buy some florist's picks, or make them yourself. They are 6-inch green sticks with fine wire attached. Hold a pick against three or four flowers, wind the wire around the stems, and then insert the stick into your arrangement.

How to Handle Fragile Stems in Flower Arranging

Use Oasis as I described on page 97. Before you insert a fragile stem, poke the hole for the stem with a toothpick. Otherwise you'll break your stem.

How to Hold Pansies Firmly in an Arrangement

Fill your container to within an inch of the top with sand. Make holes for the pansy stems with a nut pick or a pencil, and then push the sand around the stems once they are in place.

How to Use Short-Stemmed and Long-Stemmed
Flowers in the Same Arrangement

Here's where my D.T.A.A. (don't throw away anything) rule can be really helpful. If you've followed it and saved everything that can hold soil or water, you've probably saved your tubular pill bottles. If not, start. Save especially the plastic ones. Then, when you're faced with the problem of arranging short-stemmed flowers with long-stemmed beauties, simply get out a pill bottle and wire it to a stick the length you want your flowers to be. Thin bamboo stakes

and chopsticks are excellent for this purpose. Fill the pill bottle with water, put your short-stemmed flowers in it, and then place it in your arrangement.

How to Stop Flower Holders from Slipping

Those pin holders you find so very handy for holding flowers in your containers have a tendency to slip while you're making your arrangement. If you haven't any florist's clay handy, use melted candle wax or good old chewing gum (chewed, of course).

By the way, never use florist's clay on silver or pewter. Use candle wax or paraffin. Melt the wax and then let it cool until slightly thickened before putting it on both the container and the pin holder.

Great Idea for Keeping Flowers Upright in a Vase

If you don't have chicken wire handy and your vase is tall and wide as well as handsome, simply fill it with bunches of privet, hemlock fern, yew or similar greens. Cut the greens level with the top of your container so they won't be seen, and insert your flowers. They will stay in position, I promise you.

How to Get Rid of Smelly Flower Containers

The most beautiful things in the world have the smelliest stems once they are in water for any length of time. (I guess we can't have everything.) If your vase still stinks long after you've thrown the stems out, fill it with a mixture of vinegar, salt and water. Use ½ cup of vinegar to 3 cups of water and 1 tablespoon of salt. Use less water and more vinegar and salt when the odor is really bad. Soak for about 24 hours, then scrub well in hot, sudsy water.

Keep Your Flower Water Smelling Nice

Some flower leaves pollute the water they are in. Roses, marigolds, and chrysanthemums are the worst offenders. They not only foul the water, they weaken the stems, too. The way to avoid all that is to strip stems of all their leaves before putting them in water. The best way to strip rose stems is with a wad of newspaper. What's more, stripping the thorns allows the rose to absorb more water.

Another Way to Wash Vases

Add a little ammonia to the water when you wash your vases. You'll be surprised how much longer the next bouquet of flowers will last.

What to Do with Alabaster

If you're big on arrangements, sooner or later you'll come across an alabaster vase that you feel you must have for flowers. Don't put water in it as it is, or it will eventually disintegrate. Instead, pour some melted wax into it and turn it gently until all inside surfaces are coated. Then you can add your water.

What to Do with Gray Clay

Most floral-arranging clay is a dirty gray color. If you don't like the looks of it (I certainly don't; it looks awful in a beautiful arrangement), color it brown by working instant coffee into it . . . if you can afford coffee these days.

Fruit and Flowers Sometimes Don't Mix

When fruits such as apples, bananas, peaches and avocados are kept in the same room as daffodils or carnations, the flowers take a beating. These particular fruits give out ethylene gas, which can cause the drooping and withering of the flowers. Fruit can reduce a carnation to a shrunken head. Roses, too, can be harmed by the gas, but to a lesser degree. Play it safe. Keep the fruits away from your flower arrangements.

How to Become an Instant Garden Expert

Do you know who introduced formal flower arranging into the United States? Martha Washington, that's who.

Give Green Pears That Rosy Glow

Pears make a nice table centerpiece, and they'll last longer if you buy them green. To give them that rosy glow, rub a little lipstick on them.

TIPS ON FLOWER AND LEAF DRYING

What to Use and How to Dry Flowers

In every seed catalog you'll find a group of flowers labeled "everlastings." They're the flowers that hold their shape and color when dried, and they are indeed lovely in arrangements, shadow boxes or framed pictures. Some of the best varieties are helichrysum, yarrow, strawflowers, globe amaranth, blue salvia, limonium, goldenrod and honesty.

Drying them is as easy as growing them. The trick is to cut the flowers before they are fully open, then remove the leaves and hang the flowers heads down in an airy location. Let them dry slowly and never over artificial heat. Bells of Ireland, celosia and baby's breath, while not in the everlasting class, can also be dried this way to last a long, long time. (If I had been appointed Mother Nature, I would have had all flowers last this way—at least through the winter.)

More About Drying Flowers

Try these flowers, too, for air-drying. They turn out well and also last throughout the entire winter. Yarrow (*Achillea*) should be cut when all the individual florets have opened and the entire head is bright yellow. Strip leaves and hang flowers six to eight to a bunch. Secure stems with a rubber band. Dusty miller (*Artemisia*) can be cut at any time right up to the first frost. Both flowers and foliage dry well. Baptisia (*B. australis*) should not be cut until the pealike seed pods have turned blue-black. You don't have to strip the leaves. Hang in small bunches.

Here's Some More

Add these to your list of flowers that dry well when hung in a dark, dry, cool, airy room: Chinese lantern, Job's-tears, larkspur, Queen Anne's lace. Pick them at the time of day when they are perfectly dry and then remove all foliage. Tie them upside down in bunches to coat hangers and hang them up to dry.

More Ideas for Air-Drying Specific Flowers

Globe thistle should be cut before any florets on the head open. If they are cut after the florets open, the steel-blue globes tend to disintegrate when dry.

Love-in-a-mist has seedpods that are ideal for drying. They are oval-shaped balloons covered with green fuzz. Wait until all the pods have formed, and then cut the whole plant and hang.

Not only is okra good to eat, but it dries well, too. Wait until the pod has become quite hard and is way past being edible. Cut the stems with groups of pods, strip the leaves and hang.

Salvia should be cut before the florets of the spike open.

Strip off any excess leaves and tie in bunches of twenty-five. Hang.

Jewels of Opar should be cut after the headlike seedpods have formed. Since the stem is leafless, hang about twenty to a bunch.

How to Hold Dried Arrangements in Place

Fill your containers with sand or vermiculite. Wet thoroughly and pack down. After the material dries it will be stronger and better able to hold stems, because it will be packed down tighter than if you had used the same substance as it came from the package.

How to Keep a Dried Arrangement in Place Permanently

I think you'll like this secret. It's been so useful to me. After your dried arrangement is just the way you want it—with the stems tucked neatly into the sand or vermiculite—hold it securely in place by pouring melted wax around and in between the flower stems.

Another Flower-Arranging Secret

Keep seeds from dropping into your dried arrangements by spraying the flowers with hair spray.

Making Woody Material Supple

Simply boil woody material such as palm pods for several hours. That will make it supple enough to shape and bend to your fancy.

How to Make Pin Holders Really Work in
*   Dried Arrangements*

Dip the stems of your dried material in warm wax. The wax will make the stems thicker, and they will adhere more securely to the pin holder.

How to Dry Flowers That Won't Dry in the Air

How would you like to have magnificent rosebuds, zinnias, marigolds, dahlias and a lot of other summer flowers in your home all winter long? You can with what I think is the best development for flowers in our lifetime. It's something called silica gel. It can dry almost anything that grows. It takes all the moisture out of flowers and decorative leaves. It comes in cans, and it's best to buy the largest size.

You cut your flowers during the day when they are dry. Leave only a 1-inch stem, and place the flowers, one at a time, in the silica gel in layers. The way you put them into the can is the way they will dry, so be very careful how you place the petals. There's no shrinkage. Most flower colors are retained; some come out slightly darkened. All come out breathtakingly alive-looking after a week or two in the airtight can.

I put wire stems on each dried flower, cover the wire with green florist's tape, and arrange the flowers in containers, using either live or artificial greens. When dried correctly, even if uncreatively, the arrangements look as though they just came from your florist, and they stay that way all winter long. But the minute the weather becomes humid, they droop and die. Remember the beautiful young-looking woman who lived in Shangri-la and was generations old? The moment she left Shangri-la, she shriveled up and died. Well, that's what flowers that have been dried in silica gel do when the house becomes humid. After your flowers are done, you must take them out of the can and place them in an area that is absolutely humidity-free and leave them there until late fall—or whenever the sticky humid days end in your area. I put mine next to my oil furnace, which is always warm enough to keep humidity out of the cellar.

How to Do the Same Thing at Less Cost

Try that almost absorbent stuff you put in your kitty box for you-know-what. I have a friend who gets remarkable results when she dries her flowers in the kitty litter. She uses it the same way I use silica gel. I think my colors come out better, but my pocketbook doesn't.

Drying Wildflowers

Experiment yourself and you'll soon find out which flowers dry best. Generally, goldenrod and wild aster, if picked at their peak, will retain their color when air-dried. In late summer, blooms of joe-pye weed are excellent if they are cut before the florets open and their leaves are stripped before bunching. Try dock with its brown seed heads as well as the upright mullein.

Use Rubber Bands for Drying Flowers

When you hang up your flowers in a cool place to dry, use rubber bands rather than string or twist-'ems to hold the stems together.

The stems shrink when they dry, and the rubber bands contract with the stems and prevent the flowers from falling.

How to Hold Up Dried Flowers

Many people dry the stems along with the flowers. I don't. I leave about ½-inch of real stem, and then when the flower is dried, I tape a wire stem to the real one. This makes the flower stand up far better in an arrangement. However, if you are determined to dry the stem, use sand or gravel rather than styrofoam to hold your arrangement.

How to Preserve Branches for Arrangements

Magnolia, laurel, beech, dogwood, salal and lemon branches preserve marvelously with a glycerin-and-water treatment. Naturally you should choose the most attractive and well-shaped branches, and then wash them and their leaves thoroughly with cold water. Make a solution of 1 part glycerin (buy it at the drugstore) to 2 parts water. Put the stems in the solution, making sure you put at least 6 inches of stem into it. Set the container in a warm, dark area. You won't see any color change for a week to 10 days. The entire "leathering" can take as long as 2 months, but it's worth it. As the branches sop up the glycerin-and-water mixture, their leaves turn either golden, dark brown or bronze, depending on the kind of branch it is.

Make sure there is enough solution in the containers, since some of the branches will absorb a large quantity of the glycerin solution in a short time. On the slow ones, recut the stems about once a week, removing from ½ to 1 inch each time. This hurries the absorption. You'll be able to judge for yourself when the leaves are done. Once done, the branches can be used in dry arrangements, since they no longer need water to survive. They can also be used with fresh flowers. Water will not hurt their stems. Incidentally, try doing ivy in the glycerin-and-water solution. Sink the ivy completely in a half-and-half solution of glycerin and water. Results are lovely.

How to Make Pressed Leaves Even Prettier

The secret is to brush them lightly with a nonsalty oil such as olive oil before you press them.

Another Secret for Prettier Pressed Leaves

If you press the flowers and leaves between sheets of paper—any kind of paper, be it newspaper, tissue or the telephone book—change the paper every 12 hours the first 2 days. If you don't, the moisture absorbed by the paper will seep back into the foliage.

How to Take the Skunk Out of Skunk Cabbage

One of the first plants to come to life in the spring is the skunk cabbage. Its leaves and flowers are quite interesting, but who needs that smell? You can de-scent it by removing the stamens and submerging the blooms in ice water for about an hour. Keep the stems of the plant in cold water until you're going to use it. The flowers take on interesting forms as they dry and curl. When dried completely, they can be used in winter bouquets.

How to Make Your Own Towels and Washcloths from a Gourd

Ever hear of the luffa? It's a tropical gourd, a member of the cucumber family that you can grow as far north as Connecticut, and even farther north if you start it indoors in February or March. It is worth growing. The luffa is probably the least known but most amazing vegetable we have the good fortune to have. Its fibrous interior makes excellent pot holders, door mats, table mats, filters, and particularly washcloths. It is excellent—repeat, excellent—for your skin and your entire body.

During World War II, the U.S. Navy used luffa for filters in steam engines, preferring it to any other material. The army used luffa for wiping windshields of jeeps, and even for some surgical operations. In several parts of the world, luffa is used as a medicine for hundreds of different kinds of ailments. And you can also eat luffa like a cucumber. You can eat its leaves, too. Or it can be cooked in any way squash can. It can be used in soup like okra. There is so much material and lore about the luffa, I could write pages about it. Needless to say, I find it one of the world's most interesting plants. *Luffa cylindrica* is the more popular of the two species, and its fruits (gourds) can grow up to 20 inches long and weigh up to 5 pounds. Follow the directions on the seed packet for planting, and pick the gourds when the stems turn yellow. Grow the vine on a trellis or fence, and try to keep the gourds off the ground by placing stones or plastic sheeting under them.

Everyone seems to have his own method for making luffa sponges and other goodies. It's the inside of the plant you want—a mass of spongy tissue that can be shaped as you desire. Here's one way to get to that stage. The tough luffa skin can be removed by soaking the gourd until the skin peels off easily. To do that, put the luffa in a tub of water, weighting it down with a roasting pan filled with rocks. Every several days, change the water. After the skin comes off, remove the seed and shape the sponge. Try making a washcloth first. Clean it thoroughly with soap and water and then dry it in the sun for several days. It will be stiff, but will soften when used for washing. Your bath will be a stimulating experience. Luffa costs a bundle to buy, so grow your own. It'll be more fun, and it will save you money, too.

Luffa seeds are hard to find, but they are available at:

Nichols Garden Nursery
    1190 North Pacific Highway, Albany, Oregon 97321
Henry Field Seed and Nursery Co.
    Shenandoah, Louisiana 51601
Gurney Seed and Nursery Co.
    Yankton, South Dakota 57078

FIXING FADING FLOWERS FROM FRIENDLY FLORISTS

What to Do with Wilted Florist's Violets

First thing you do is wrap the stems in wax paper to protect them from the warmth of your hand. Then hold the flower heads in cold water for several minutes until they freshen up. Recut the stems and put into cold water.

How to Keep a Corsage After You've Worn It

Remove ribbons and other trimmings, and submerge the flowers (all except orchids and sweet peas) in cold water for 15 to 30 minutes. When the petals are crisp, lift out and shake off the water. Cover lightly with dampened cotton and then wrap loosely in foil, pinching the edges of the foil to seal the package. Keep in the refrigerator and you'll be able to get at least another day's wear out of it.

If your corsage is made of orchids or sweet peas, put the stems of the flowers in cold water in a container that will keep the blooms above the water. Store in the warmest location in your refrigerator, if possible at 50°.

MAKING YOUR OWN CUTTINGS

How to Root in Water

Roots like to grow in the dark. If your bottle or jar is plain glass, paint it black or any other color before you put your cuttings in. Monthly, put a little liquid fertilizer in the water, or a pinch of powdered fertilizer.

How to Root Ivy

If you root ivy in water, you shouldn't try to grow it in soil. Chances are it won't live. However, if you intend to keep it in water for a touch of greenery in an arrangement, fine and dandy. Otherwise, root ivy in sand or a mixture of vermiculite and perlite. It stands a better chance of surviving when rooted this way.

How to Make Rooting Easier

Often cuttings won't root because there are too many chemicals in your tap water. Catch some rainwater and see what a difference that makes.

Make Your Own Hormones

When you want to root plants, it is always best to use hormones to protect the plant you're propagating and encourage a root system to form. Well, root hormones, like everything else, cost money. By dumb luck, I discovered a plant that seems to produce these root hormones. The plant is coleus. By the process of elimination, I found that when hard-to-root plants are put in the same water with a cutting of coleus, which roots easily, the magic takes place. Try it. Maybe you'll have the same luck.

Safe Way to Root African Violets

There are times when you want so much to root an African violet leaf, but you have only one or two leaves—and that's when you goof. Well, you won't goof if you use this method. Fill a drinking glass to the top with water. Cover the top with aluminum foil. Make a hole

in the foil so that the leaf stalk can stand in the water while the leaf remains on the foil. As you know, if you get that leaf wet, it will be the end of your African beauty.

How to Make Cactus Cuttings That Take

This is a great secret that works equally well with geranium cuttings. When you cut a succulent, like a Christmas cactus or a hen-and-chickens or any other attractive cactus, keep it out of the rooting medium for a day or so. The cut end will "heal" or callous, and this will prevent rotting when you root it.

How to Propagate Your Own Blueberries

Sometimes this works, sometimes it doesn't, but it certainly is worth a try. In February, cut a twig about 4 or 5 inches long off your blueberry bush. Plant it in peat moss and make sure the container has bottom heat. If all is perfect, it will root and *voilà!*—blueberries. In about 5 years.

A Hint About Air Layering

The success comes from making the root-wrap airtight. And I mean airtight.

Plastic Boxes and Pans for Cuttings

My motto, as you may have realized, is don't throw away anything that can still hold something. It can always be used if you're a gardener. Case in point: those plastic dishpans and shoe and sweater boxes. They're great for holding cuttings—especially the larger ones. Punch several ½-inch drainage holes about 2 inches from the top of the pan or box. Now pour in perlite up to the drainage holes (you can buy perlite at any garden supply store). Cover the top 2 inches with a peat moss and perlite mix. Water. Put in your cuttings. Enjoy.

Easy Rooting Method

Use the pot you want to grow your plant in. Fill it with your potting soil. Then with a dowel or any kind of stick—even a broomstick—make a deep hole. Fill that hole with clean sand. Put the cutting in the sand and add water. The cutting will root quickly in the sand, and the roots will find the soil without your doing a darn thing. Depending upon the size of your pot, you can make holes for two or three cuttings.

Secret way to bring a man to his knees: grow crabgrass.

STEFANIE MULLALLY

Chapter Five

Vegetable, Fruit and Herb Garden Secrets

HOW TO GROW FOOD
GOOD ENOUGH TO EAT

ALL ABOUT AMERICA'S MOST POPULAR
VEGETABLE—A FRUIT

Be an Instant Garden Expert

Did you know that if it weren't for the U.S. Supreme Court, the tomato would never have been called a vegetable? It would have been called a fruit, which it really is. In 1893, the Court ruled that the tomato is a vegetable, after an importer claimed that tomatoes were fruits and therefore not subject to duty. The importer was really correct—botanically, that is. But the government evidently wanted duty more than accuracy. The botanical definition of a fruit is a matured ovary. Tomatoes, green peppers, snap and green beans, eggplants and the like are all fruits according to that definition.

According to a Gallup poll, the tomato is the most popular vegetable and Brussels sprouts the least.

Be the First on Your Block to Have Ripe Tomatoes

Here's a sensational idea for early tomatoes or early anything else—but especially tomatoes. It's a cage—an honest-to-goodness wire cage with a plastic cover—which you can make yourself easily at little cost. What's more, you can use it again and again as the years go by. With this cage you don't have to prune or stake your plants. It will not only protect the tomatoes from heavy winds and storms in early summer, but it will also give you clean, healthy fruit later in the season that never touches the ground because the branches can be trained to grow through the mesh. I urge you to make at least one cage.

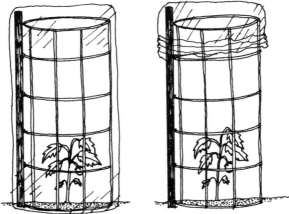

Here's how you do it. Using 4 x 4-inch mesh wire, make the cages about 4 feet high and as wide as the largest heavy weight clear plastic bag you can scrounge from your cleaners. Staple a 4½- to 5-foot pointed stick to one end in order to anchor the cage to the ground. Twist the loose ends on each side into hooks, and hook the sides together. You can unhook the cage at the end of the season to store it flat. After you have made your cylinder and anchored it to the ground, put your plastic bag over the entire cage. Pull the plastic up on warm sunny days, and down on cold blustery ones.

Try just one cage and I'll bet you'll have a gardenful the following year. You will have carefree tomatoes, as well as earlier crops—often by 3 or 4 weeks. Utopia.

Another Way to Get Earlier Tomatoes

When planting, dig the hole a little deeper than usual and throw in a shovelful of hot manure (fresh, not aged), then a shovelful of soil, and then the tomato plant. The extra layer of soil will prevent the tomato roots from burning, and the rising heat from the decomposing manure will warm the soil, giving your plant faster growth, and, therefore, earlier tomatoes.

How to Tell When Tomatoes Should Be Planted if You're Doing It the Regular Way

Take the soil's temperature. You can do it with any outdoor thermometer with an exposed bulb or mercury end. Plant tomatoes only when the temperature of the top 2 inches of soil is above 55°F at a noon reading.

No-Cost Care for Tomato Plants

In the spring we're all so anxious to set out those tomato plants that we forget that the weather can get cold even after it's been warm and springlike. Tomatoes cannot stand those very cold early spring nights unless you take some precautions. Try this. Save your half-gallon milk cartons, slice off both the bottoms and the tops and insert a carton into the soil around each tomato plant. Leave them

there until you're sure spring is really here to stay. The cartons will protect your tender little plants from not only the cold but also the sun and wind, and they will thrive.

Increase the Sex Life of Your Tomatoes

Often humid weather slows the setting of fruit. Even in perfect weather, tomato blossoms and bees are sometimes slow in doing what should come naturally. So, you can make like Mother Nature by shaking the plants at midday when the humidity is low. If your tomatoes are tied to stakes, shake the stakes. Shaking releases the pollen, in case you don't know much about the sex life of tomatoes.

More Show-off Facts

Did you know that one mature tomato plant gives off one gallon of water on a dry day? What's more, in one growing season a single tomato plant requires 349 gallons of water, one corn plant 54 gallons, and one sunflower plant 130 gallons. Guzzlers all.

How to Tell a Sucker on a Plant

It's best to nip off tomato suckers as they come out—and that's almost daily—if you want larger tomatoes. Some people nip off the bloom stem, and that means no tomatoes. Just remember that the suckers are always directly at the leaf axils. The yellow clusters that are always on the main stem between leaf joints are, in case you didn't know, the beginnings of your tomatoes.

Free Tomato Plants All Season Long

This is a secret every tomato grower should try. Instead of pinching off all the suckers from your tomato plants, let some of them grow to a length of 12 inches. Then cut them and plant them about 4 inches deep, and they'll form roots along the entire buried stem. The deeper they are planted, the stronger the plant will be. Keep the ground moist, and shield your bonanza from the direct rays of the sun until the roots take hold. Another bonus, courtesy of Mother Nature.

What to Do with Leggy Tomatoes

Sometimes the tomato plants you get at garden centers are leggy (or tall and spindly), but don't let that bother you. When you plant a leggy plant, lay it on its side and cover the leggy part with soil. It is a good rule always to plant tomatoes as deep as the lower leaf stem.

Another Interesting Fact

Do you know what country was the first to report the existence of the tomato? Italy, of course (maybe that's why tomatoes and Italian cooking are synonymous). In 1544. The first report of the tomato in North America was in the Carolinas in 1710.

Would You Believe Sun Is Not Good for Tomatoes?

It isn't, after you pick them. Of course, they should be picked when they are fully vine ripened, but if you do pick them before, put them in the shade to ripen, because even partial sunlight causes uneven ripening.

Grow Tomatoes in a Laundry Basket

I have a friend whose only garden is her terrace, which covers two sides of her apartment house. She gets sun on one side in the morning and on the other side in the afternoon. She likes to grow tomatoes, but she has to move them each day in order to follow the sun. What does she do? She grows them in laundry baskets, which are easier to carry than a big redwood planter. Neat idea. Here's how you can do what she does: line the basket with a large heavy-duty plastic garbage bag, fill it almost to the top with soil, and then let the soil settle for a day or two. Pierce a few holes in the bottom of the plastic for drainage. Plant the tomato deep—up to the first leaves. Stake it and water. You can do the same thing with pepper, eggplant, small vined cucumbers or a bush-type string bean. Experiment and *bon appetit.*

When to Pick Green Tomatoes

When the cold weather silences the crickets, that's when.

When to Pick Green Tomatoes if the Crickets Don't Cooperate

Try katydids. The first katydid is announcing six more growing weeks before frost. If you're not a believer, test this theory by making a note of when you heard the first katydid. Keep track and see whether it is indeed six weeks before the first day of frost or whether this is a myth like the groundhog and his shadow.

How to Ripen Tomatoes

Some people put them in a brown paper bag in a cool spot indoors. I prefer to wrap each one in tissue paper or newspaper and place them in boxes in a cool place. This way I have tomatoes right up to Thanksgiving.

Tomatoes for Your Skin

You may end up smelling like a salad, but tomatoes are a good skin cleanser and can help your skin get rid of excess oil. Or so I've been told by some pretty cute tomatoes (the two-legged kind). You rub a wedge of fresh tomato over your entire face and throat, and then allow the liquid to remain on your skin until it dries. Rinse in cool water and pat dry. You might feel some tingling when you slop a tomato on your face this way, but this is stimulating and good for your skin. If your skin feels dry after your tomato treatment, put a little cream or oil on it.

AND NOW FOR THE REAL VEGETABLES

You Can Grow Vegetables Almost Anywhere

If you only have a flower bed, you still can have an edible border, and one that looks good, too. Parsley makes a lovely green border and foreground for your flowers. Chives, too, make a nice edging. Be creative. There are many herbs that will also look good among your flowers. Study the pictures of the different vegetables and herbs. You'll find many decorative ones. Flowering cabbage and kale are spectacular.

How to Plant by the Moon

If you believe in regulating your activities according to the moon, try this: for crops that bear their vegetables above the ground, plant during a waxing moon (from new to full). Plant below-the-ground crops such as potatoes, beets and other root vegetables during the waning moon (from full to new). And as for you people who scoff at this stuff—don't knock it until you try it.

Ripen Vegetables Faster

This secret is from the U.S. Department of Agriculture and it's a goody. Use aluminum foil at the feet of your tomato, melon or squash plants, especially when there hasn't been much sunshine. The reflection from the foil gives off extra light and hurries the ripening process. The foil over the soil also prevents weed growth.

A Brilliant Way to Keep Weeds Down in a Vegetable Garden

This is really ingenious. Make a vegetable garden out of strips in your lawn. Not your front lawn, but an out-of-the-way area. First, measure the width of your lawn mower or lawn spreader (whichever is wider). Let's say it's 3 feet. Okay, leave 3 feet of lawn the length of your plot. Then dig a trench 1 foot wide, the length of your plot. Now leave 3 feet more of lawn, then dig another 1-foot-wide trench. Keep doing this until you have used up all your space. Of course, you don't have as much space to grow vegetables if you try this, but for someone who doesn't need much space and hates to weed, this sure fills the bill. If you use black plastic to line the trenches, you'll hardly see a weed. All you have to do is cut your lawn and pick the vegetables.

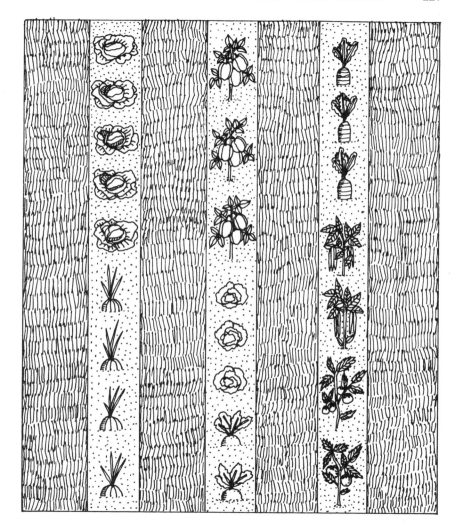

Trick for Planting Onions

Use an old dinner fork to make openings in the soil. Plant onion or shallot set (that's the bulblet), but do not press it into the soil. If onion set is pressed in or forced, the soil under it gets hard, and the growing root system will push the onion head out of the ground.

How to Make Homegrown Onions Last Longer

Store your onions in nylon stockings. Drop them in one at a time, tying a knot in the stocking after each onion. When the stocking is full, hang it in a cool room. When you want one onion, just cut below a knot and remove the onion from its individual "package." This is an excellent way to store onions, because they demand "solitary confinement." They spoil faster when thrown together.

Free Onions

It's pretty annoying to buy onions at the supermarket and find after opening the bag that many have sprouted. It's even more annoying to the owners of supermarkets. They have to throw away many bags because the customers won't buy sprouted onions. Ask the manager for some of these bags—free—and plant the sprouted onions in the garden. Once the tops have died down, gather the tiny bulbs and plant them about 3 inches apart. Result—real honest-to-goodness onions, courtesty of your supermarket.

How to Get More Lettuce from Lettuce

This is a useful trick. Harvest your lettuce as the plant grows. In other words, take a few leaves from each plant as it is growing. The plant will then grow more leaves, and you'll get a succession of fresh leaves—sort of a bonus—for at least a month.

Gladiolus, Enemy of Peas and Beans

Gladiolus, for some reason I cannot explain, has an inhibiting effect on the growth of peas and beans even when they are grown as far as 50 feet away. The peas and beans grow, but they just don't grow as well.

Special Secret for Growing Carrots

Carrots need a loose, sandy, well-drained soil. If you don't have it, don't give up carrots; just drink a lot of coffee. Then work coffee grounds into the soil. It will loosen the soil and make it the way carrots like it. Not only that, but the coffee grounds will protect the carrots from most insects.

Try White Carrots for a Change. You Might Even Fool the Bunnies

There really is a white carrot. The seeds are hard to find, but you can buy them from Nichols Garden Nursery, 1190 North Pacific Highway, Albany, Oregon 97321.

Carrot Tops for Salads

When you grow your own carrots, you get those feathery green tops which you don't usually get on the carrots you buy at the supermarket. Fresh carrot tops are good in salads and soups, and make a decorative, edible garnish just like parsley.

Beat the High Cost of Snow Peas

Grow them. They're easy to grow, and they cost a small fortune to buy at the supermarket. If you cook Chinese food you need a lot of them. In catalogs they are called "Edible Podded Peas." Get the variety called dwarf gray sugar, which matures in 65 days. The pod is bite size.

Snow peas are very generous producers, and you get almost double the amount you get from the same number of shell pea plants. They also have fewer calories. Seeds are available from most seedmen. I recommend dwarf gray sugar because it needs no staking and is ideal where space is limited and the season is short.

Two Cabbages for the Price of One

You can get two heads of cabbage from one plant if you play your cards carefully. Cut out the head, leaving the big outer leaves. When the second growth comes in, it will be in the form of eight or nine little sprouts coming out of the center. Remove all but one. That one will be your next head of cabbage. Aren't we sneaky fooling Mother Nature this way?

Get More Light in Your Garden

If you have a part of the garden that needs more light for the plants you're growing, play God and make your own light. Glue

aluminum foil on large sheets of plywood to make a king-sized re-
flector. You'll get a lot of free additional light where most needed.

How to Make Pumpkin Seeds Edible

Don't wash off that pulp that clings to the seeds—they'll get
slimy and mold quickly. Pull out as much of the pumpkin's interior as
you can, and then spread the whole gooky mess on a baking sheet.
Put the baking sheet on top of a warm oven or into a cooling oven.
The seeds will dry in a few days. When they are dry, toast them in the
oven and sprinkle a little salt on them. Delicious.

How to Hull Sunflower Seeds

Put the seeds in boiling water for a few minutes and the
shells will come off much more easily. You can also use pliers to crack
them. Lay the seed between the pliers as you would between your
teeth so it can be cracked lengthwise.

The Answer to Potatoes When You're Dieting

Ever hear of the Jerusalem artichoke? It isn't an artichoke,
and it isn't from Jerusalem. It's a tuber that grows like a potato but is
completely without starch. It has a crisp, nutty flavor and can be
served in place of potato. It stores its carbohydrates in the form of
inulin (not insulin) and its sugar in the form of levulose. Anybody
dieting should grow it because of its small number of calories: seven
calories per 100 grams (between 3 and 4 ounces) of freshly dug prod-

uct. Seventy-five calories per 100 grams if the Jerusalem artichoke has been stored for a long period. It's one of the easiest of all vegetables to grow—and one plant will produce many small, very edible tubers.

The Jerusalem artichoke belongs to the daisy family, and its name is a corruption of the Italian *girasole,* meaning sunflower. It is a native of North America and was used as food by the Indians.

How to Grow Jerusalem Artichokes

Plant them just as you do potatoes, but remember that they are perennials, so the spot where you put them will be a permanent one. Their small sunflower blossoms grow on stalks that reach anywhere from 6 to 12 feet high. You must, therefore, plant them where they won't shade the rest of your garden. They yield better than potatoes and are handled and harvested the same way, but they don't store as well as potatoes. However, you can leave them in the ground throughout the winter under a heavy mulch and dig them up during thaws—if you've got the muscle. Otherwise, store them like potatoes.

What You May Not Know About Sweet Potatoes

Sweet potatoes don't get much publicity, and yet one medium-sized sweet potato will give you 33% of the minimum daily requirement of vitamin C and a whopping 150% of the adult requirement of vitamin A. If you boil them in their jackets, peel and serve quickly and you won't lose much vitamin C.

Keep the Starch Out of Your Corn

The sugar in corn quickly changes to starch unless the corn is refrigerated immediately after picking. Eat your corn immediately after picking, or buy corn that has been kept cold.

How to Pick Green Peppers

Leave about an inch of stem when you pick peppers. You'll find that they'll be crisper and have more life, even after they're stored in the refrigerator.

Growing Turnips in Limited Space

In a small vegetable garden, grow them between corn.

Vegetables That Will Grow in the Shade

Most vegetables need to be grown in full sun. But there are some that can do well in partial shade. Lettuce, garden peas and cucumbers will grow in partial shade, but don't push your luck with cukes. Give them as much sun as you can, or lay aluminum foil on the soil to double their sun while the sun is out, and double their light when it isn't.

Grow Your Own Sugar

If you grow sugar beets, you can make your own sugar and blackstrap molasses, too. Several seed companies sell the seed. Instructions for the home refining of sugar come with each package. Two large roots, when boiled, will produce a cup of sugar and half a cup of blackstrap molasses. This was a great favorite in grandma's day for everything that ailed you in the spring.

Freeze Vegetables Neatly

Here's a great idea for freezing fresh vegetables. Put your plastic bags inside milk cartons, and then you can stack them in your freezer more neatly than you could stack the bags themselves. You'll save space, and you won't have the bags falling out every time you open the freezer door.

KEEPING RABBITS AND RACCOONS IN THEIR PLACE—ANYWHERE BUT IN YOUR GARDEN

How to Keep Raccoons Away

Raccoons aren't as smart as they think they are. You can fence them out of your garden with chicken wire—and you won't need much, because raccoons aren't able to think out a problem. Staple 24-inch-wide wire to 12-inch posts. Raccoons, you see, never dig under fences; they climb over them. As soon as they climb this fence, their weight will bring the slack top over on top of them and scare the you-know-what out of them.

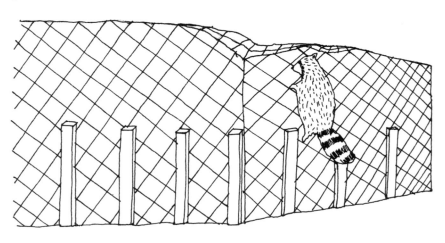

How to Keep Rabbits Out of the Vegetable Garden—Maybe

Try mothballs. Scatter them along the rows of plants. (Squirrels don't like mothballs either.) If mothballs don't work on the rabbits, dust plants with sulfur, powdered lime, dried blood or powdered alum mixed with wheat flour. If you can get tobacco dust, use it instead of wheat flour. Or try dusting the plants at the edge of your garden with red pepper. Take your pick.

ENJOYING THE FRUIT OF YOUR LABOR

When to Pick a Pear

They ripen best off the tree. Pick them while the fruit is still very firm and just turning yellowish green. Pears develop their best flavor when left sitting at room temperature (65°to 70°).

When to Pick a Cantaloupe

One way, besides using your nose, is to look for a smooth stem. That means the cantaloupe is ready to be plucked. Some people tell by color, but the sure-proof way is by smell. If it smells like a cantaloupe, it's ripe. Incidentally, the sugar content does not increase after it is picked, as some people think.

When to Pick Fruits for Jelly

If you're going to use concentrated pectin, pick your fruits and berries when they are firm and ripe. If you're making your own pectin, slightly underripe fruit is best.

How to Get Peaches to Ripen

Often store-bought peaches are so hard and inedible you could put a hex on the store where you bought them. Here's a better idea, and one that will get results. Put the peaches in a brown paper bag along with an apple. The apple will release ethylene gas and ripen the peaches in a couple of days. Beats eating them green.

How to Grow an Honest-to-Goodness Pineapple

From those wonderful people who give us Dole pineapple comes their secret way to grow pineapple. Start with a fresh pineapple. Its leafy top, called the "crown," is the part of the pineapple that makes more pineapples. Twist or cut off that crown. Trim off any adhering fruit or flesh. Strip off three or four basal leaves (they're the leaves at the base of the crown).

Place the crown upside down in a dry, shady place for a week. The cut end and the leaf scars will harden to help prevent rot. After the week is over, start your pineapple with the foliage up in an 8-inch porous clay pot. Use a good light garden soil and mix in about 30% of well-composted organic matter, leaf mold or peat moss. Be sure your pot has good drainage. Pineapples do not like to have wet feet. Firm the soil around the base without getting any of it on the leaves in the crown. Fertilize every two or three months and give it lots of sun. Remember, the pineapple is a tropical plant. Frost or freezing temperatures will kill it.

In Hawaii, a pineapple takes from 24 to 26 months to produce a ripe fruit. Yours may take longer. In about 16 months a bud will form in the center of the leaves, but you won't be able to see it until a bright red cone appears around it in 18 months. Then bright blue flowers will appear. If, however, after 20 months it has not flowered, put the entire plant into a solid plastic bag (one with no air holes). Put a red apple in the bag and tie the bag closed. (Sounds like witchcraft.) Place it in a shady spot for three days, and then take the plant out of the bag and return it to its usual sunny location. After two months, the bright red cone will appear. The bright blue flowers will then open row by row over the next two weeks. When the petals of the last flower have dried, the fruit will begin to develop. When the fruit is about 6 months old, it is sweet enough to eat. Unless you're too old by this time to eat it!

Grow Your Own Palm Tree

Save those date pits and put them on the kitchen windowsill to dry. In about two weeks, plant them. In about three weeks you should see signs of life. Then, in a couple of months, the leaves should begin to appear. Palm does best in the sun and should be watered only when the soil feels dry.

Grow Your Own Orange Tree

Seeds from breakfast oranges should be soaked in warm water until they swell. Plant in light sandy soil. Growth is slow. The plant is lovely, but don't hold your breath till you see oranges. You won't. It takes two to tango.

How to Make Peach or Apricot Leather

You know what peach or apricot leather is, don't you? If you don't, your kids sure do—and love it. It's that leathery stuff you see in the deli department of the supermarket, all rolled up and covered with see-thru wrap and sold at ridiculous prices. All it's made of is a little sugar and a lot of peaches or apricots. Marvelous thing to make yourself when you have an abundance of fresh peaches or apricots. Here's how you make it: use half a cup of sugar for each pound of peeled and stoned peaches or apricots. Bring the fruit and sugar slowly to a boil, then simmer until most of the moisture from the fruit has cooked away. Mash the fruit into a smooth paste as it cooks.

Grease a large dish or platter, and spread the mashed fruit on it in a thin sheet. Put it in the sun until thoroughly dry. If there isn't any sun, put it in your oven with only the pilot light on; or, if your stove is electric, set the temperature at its lowest setting. When the leather is thoroughly dry, roll it up, wrap it in a clean cloth and store in a cool, dry place—if your kids (or you) don't eat it first. Delicious.

How to Get More Grapes from Your Vine

I haven't tried it, but I'm told that if you plant the herb hyssop under a grapevine, it will increase the yield and quality of the grape.

How to Improve Strawberries' Flavor

Mulch your strawberry bed with pine needles. Their acid content will make the plants more vigorous and give the fruit better flavor.

Be an Instant Garden Expert

Did you know the apple was first found in Persia? In America, the first apple we have on record is the Roxbury Russet in 1649.

The Apple Has Been Falsely Accused

Did you know that the apple was not the forbidden fruit that got Eve kicked out of the Garden of Eden? The Bible doesn't say what fruit it was—it merely refers to it as "forbidden fruit." Botanists think it was probably an apricot. (The fellow who first called it an apple must have been selling apricots.)

How to Reach High Apples from the Ground

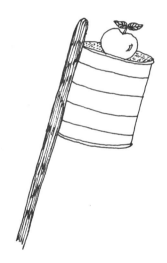

Get a big pole or a broomstick—depending on the size of your trees. Nail a large-sized juice can with an open top to the pole or broomstick. Or you could cut a plastic bleach bottle and mount it on your pole. Jiggle the can or bottle against the apple branch, and the apple will fall into the container.

How to Get Apples When Your Apple Tree
Won't Give You Any

If nature won't, you can. But first make sure there are two apple trees in your garden. This is necessary for reasons you're old enough to know. If there are two trees in full sun and you're not getting apples, try this: about the first of July, girdle or ring the trunk by cutting a one-eighth-inch-wide groove in the bark down to the cambium layer—the layer of living tissue just below the bark. Remove the bark from the groove you've cut. What this will do is slow down the movement of sugars and nutrients enough so that the amount of sugar in the top will be sufficient for the tree to set flower buds the following spring.

If your apple tree is set in the middle of your lawn, the grass fertilizer you've used may be the culprit. It may cause leaf buds to form rather than flower buds.

Dried Apple Snacks—Non-fattening Goodies

I have just discovered these goodies, and I shall be forever grateful to the lady who told me about them. They *are* the answer to the junk food we all eat, and, glory be, if they aren't as delicious as they are healthful.

Peel your apples and cut into four or five rounds per apple. Cut out cores with a doughnut cutter. Dunk the slices in rose hip tea (you buy it at any health food counter). Drain and place on towels. Then dry them out on oven racks with the oven temperature at its lowest setting. When thoroughly dry, freeze them in plastic bags—if you haven't eaten them all. Really, really good.

Lettuce and Fruit Don't Mix

Fruit—beautiful, delicious, innocent-looking fruit—is lethal to lettuce, so don't store them near each other. When they ripen, many fruits give off a gas which can cause the lettuce to develop brown spots.

Beat the Squirrels to Your Blueberries

Sprinkle mothballs near your blueberries. If possible, set them on a level with the blueberries as well as on the ground. Squirrels simply don't like the odor of mothballs.

HERBS TO TANTALIZE THE TASTE, EYE AND NOSE

About the Space You Need for an Herb Garden

Contrary to popular belief, you do not have to have a lot of room to grow more herbs than you'll need—even if you're a gourmet cook. A plot 5 feet square with full sun is all you'll need to give you a plentiful supply. Twenty square feet of almost any kind of well-drained soil is really a perfect size for an herb garden. If the soil is not well drained, mix some coarse perlite into it to aid drainage. Remember, herb gardens don't need a lot of fertilizer. Fertilizer will make the herbs greener and more beautiful, but they won't have the true-to-herb flavor they get when grown in poor soil.

Become an Instant Garden Expert

Did you know that a crown of bay leaves in very olden times was a mark of distinction? The word bachelor is derived from bay laurel, which comes from *bacca-laureus,* or laurel berry. The Romans believed bay protected them and their homes from thunderstorms.

Herb Hint

When a recipe calls for herbs, use twice as much of a fresh herb as you would of a dried one.

How to Dry Most Herbs

The trick is to make sure all dampness is removed or else mold will appear after bottling. Wash the herb, stem and all, and drain well. Put into a brown paper bag and close with a rubber band. Hang

upside down to dry in a well-ventilated room for a week or two until the leaves are dry enough to crumble. Don't be in a rush to crumble. If the leaves are not absolutely dry, a whole summer's work will have hit the dust.

How to Dry Chives and Parsley

No brown-bag routine for chives or parsley. Spread chives over a thin layer of kosher or noniodized salt on a cookie sheet. Then sprinkle more salt over the chives. Put in a 200° oven for 12 to 15 minutes. When dry and stiff, shake out the salt, crumble the chives and store in jars. Use the chive-flavored salt for cooking meats or vegetables. A serendipitous pleasure. Parsley dries best when spread out in a thin layer on a cookie sheet and put into a 400° oven for about 3 minutes. Turn it over and leave it in the oven 2 minutes more.

Be an Instant Garden Expert

Did you know mint was named for Menthe, a nymph who was loved by Pluto, the god of the underworld? When Pluto's wife found out about Menthe, she turned her into a plant—a plant that would spend an eternity seeking underground waters looking for her lost god.

Did you also know that mint comes in as many flavors as ice cream—almost? There is orange mint, peppermint, pineapple mint, spearmint, apple mint, pennyroyal and Corsican mint. Corsican mint (*Mentha requienii*) is probably the smallest flowering plant in cultivation, with the tiniest flowers I believe there are. It is a creeping plant whose stems will root as they creep. It forms a very dense carpet of pinhead leaves of bright green, with tiny light lilac-colored flowers. The nice thing about the plant is that when it is planted in flagstone paths or in sidewalk crevices, it literally fills the air with mint fragrance when stepped upon. Try it—it's fun.

The *Mint for Juleps, Jellies and Sauces*

The best mint to grow for these three gifts of life is *Mentha spicata.*

Mint for Juleps, Even in the Shade

If your plantation is shady and you like mint, don't fret or go out and buy it. Grow it in the shade. Mint does very well in the shade. In fact, mint will grow almost anyplace and under almost any conditions.

All You'll Ever Want to Know About Parsley Lore

Did you know that the winners of the Olympic Games in ancient Greece (where it all started) were given wreaths of parsley as a prize? Did you know that in A.D. 164, Galen, the Greek physician and final authority on the use of vegetables in medicine, claimed that parsley was "sweet and grateful to the stomach"? In the sixteenth century it was generally known that parsley "comforteth the heart and the stomach." In the seventeenth century it was agreed that parsley was useful to children and "upgrown people" who were troubled with "wind in the stomach."

Almost Instant Parsley

Parsley is a must for growing all year round. It thrives in the kitchen in the winter (plant it in a bulb pot so it will spread) and is a cinch to grow outdoors. It needs sun only half the day. To get it to germinate fast, soak the tiny seeds in lukewarm water. They'll germinate in 5 to 7 days. Otherwise it will take 20 days for germination.

How to Cure Your Dog's Bad Breath (and Your Own)

Mix parsley in with your dog's food. Chew on some yourself and you'll find it really works.

How to Get Rid of Insects at a Fish Fry

This is just marvelous—a simple insect-removing idea that will make you the hero or heroine of the next fish fry. Barbecue the fish over fennel branches. You'll end up with a most flavorful fish, and you won't have the little dastards bothering you. Fennel, you know, is an herb whose leaves are used in fish sauce and for garnishing.

Be an Instant Garden Expert

Did you know that in medieval times it was believed that dill provided protection from the spells of witches? Botanists think, or at least some of them do, that when the Bible refers to anise, it is really the dill plant the storytellers of olde are talking about.

Grow Dill in the Same Place Each Year

Dill self-sows easily. The curious thing is that the resulting plants are much larger and stronger than your original sowing. Don't ask me why. Just count Nature's blessings.

All You'll Ever Want to Know About Basil

I find it easier to start basil from seed in jiffy pots than to take established plants from the garden for growing indoors. When your plant is tall enough to pinch, pinch back centers to the first set of leaves. The top will grow back and the plant will bush out in quick fashion. It will be a beautiful leafy plant if blossoms are not allowed to form. Basil is an annual and is native to India. There it is carried to the funeral pyre as a passport to heaven. It was once thought of as a courting herb. A sprig of it in a boy's hat or a girl's hand meant they were in love.

How to Handle Chives

Unless you want to wait 2 years, you shouldn't grow chives from seed. It takes that long for a chive to mature. You can buy little clumps of chives in most supermarkets the minute spring is in the air. To make them go a long way, divide them, bulb by bulb, and set them 5 inches apart in your garden. If you want to grow them in a pot in your home, use a large pot or planter, and plant about 6 to 9 bulbs, depending on the size of the container. Fresh chives are great to have handy in the house in the winter. Feed the plants regularly (about twice a month) with fish emulsion.

What to Do Before You Bring in Chives

Pot your garden chives and leave them there to freeze before you bring them into the house. Freezing gives them the rest period they need in order to give you a growth that is firm and plump and fresh.

What to Do When You Bring in Your Summer Herbs

So many herb plants brown the first few weeks after they are brought in from the summer garden. The secret to a long healthy life is often the kind of pot you put them into. It must be the right size. The roots must never touch the sides of the pot. Crowded roots cause the plant to brown. It's also not good for the plant to be suspended in air or placed alone on a high stand. Then it is exposed to currents of hot air as the heat rises. Until your herbs really get acclimated to the indoors, check them every day, water them generously and let them know you care. Don't overfertilize. Three applications during the winter should be enough for most herbs.

OUTSMARTING THE BIRDS

How to Keep Birds Away from Corn

Get some 7-inch paper cups. As soon as the corn appears, slip a cup over each ear. The birds will feel frustrated, but you'll save your corn.

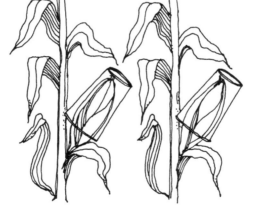

Beat the Birds to Your Strawberries

If you lay a few foot-long lengths of old garden hose among your strawberry plants, you may fool the birds into thinking they are snakes. Birds don't like snakes and will stay away. If they don't, all you've done is made a silly asp of yourself.

How to Keep Birds and Rabbits from Berries or Other Edible Plants

Save your nylon curtains and throw them over the plants or bushes you don't want your garden friends to share. The curtains won't rob your plant of light, and after the season is over you can throw them in the washing machine to make them ready for use next growing season.

Another Way to Prevent Birds from Eating Your Fruits and Berries—Sometimes

Some people have very good luck keeping birds from eating their garden fruit and berries by providing alternatives. Birds prefer wild fruit and berries, but they eat the kind you grow because there isn't anything else. Here's a list of alternatives. To protect cherries and strawberries, plant Russian mulberry or shadbush. For blackberries and raspberries, plant mulberries, elders or chokeberries. Near grapes, plant elders or Virginia creeper.

And Still Another Way to Prevent Birds from Eating Your Fruits and Berries—Sometimes

I have very good luck with cloth or aluminum foil streamers attached to cord strung across the "fruited" area. The streamers wave in the wind and scare the birds. To install, you simply have to drive stakes wherever you want protection and connect them with heavy cord fastened about 20 inches above the ground. Cut streamers from white cloth, making them about 3 inches wide and about 18 inches long. Tie them to the cord every 20 inches or so. They should just barely clear the ground. If you want to use aluminum foil, make your streamers with a hole on one end and string them through the cord.

Foil doesn't last too long, but its crackling in the wind certainly deters the birds. If you've got a Rube Goldberg kind of mind, extend the cord from your garden to your house so when there's no wind, you can jostle the cord when birds appear.

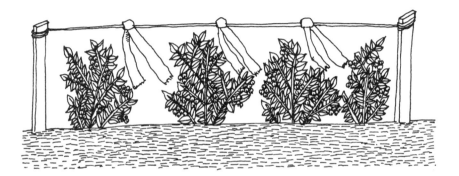

How to Scare a Crow

Pretend you're a snake. Stand in the garden and hiss like one, placing your tongue slightly behind and above your upper teeth. Hiss as loud as possible and watch the crows scatter. Better do it when no one is looking or people might think you're slightly batty.

What to Do When Grasshoppers Attack Your Vegetables

You can't use poison sprays, but you can use birds. Here's how: cut half-gallon milk cartons in half and fill the bottom half with a 10% molasses solution. Grasshoppers love molasses, so put the cartons where the infestation is at its worst. Then charm the birds with seed or bread crumbs. Once the birds get there you'll see the feast of all time: the grasshoppers eating the molasses, the birds eating the grasshoppers, and the ants eating your bread crumbs. But you won't have any more grasshoppers.

Why You Must Never Hurt a Bird

Well, one very big reason is that if we didn't have birds, we'd be up to our nostrils in insects and over our heads in weeds! In fact, without birds we might not be able to exist. For example, if just two Colorado potato beetles were allowed to increase without birds eating them, there would be over 60 million potato beetles from just the two of them at the end of a single season. And one young robin can eat 165 cutworms in a single day, almost twice its own weight. Awesome—when you think of how many cutworms and potato beetles there are in the world.

Some genius estimated that birds feed their nestlings every few minutes during the entire day. If they eat only 200 insects a day (and they probably eat more), in 15 days they destroy about 3,000 insects per nest. Get the picture? Without birds, we simply would not exist. Take care of them, because they take care of us.

Plants That Attract Birds

Catbirds, cardinals and thrashers like chokeberry, dogwood, mulberry, hawthorn, bush honeysuckle, barberry, yews (the kind that have berries), cotoneaster and viburnum. Birds that eat seed (mainly weed seed) are goldfinches, purple finches, chirping and song sparrows, and cardinals. The hummingbirds like flowers such as columbine, canna, pink or red monarda, scarlet sage, trumpet vine and red or pink flowering honeysuckle. Needless to say, this list of bird-attracting plants is not complete, but it's a good start.

OUTWITTING THE LITTLE DASTARDS

How to Keep Flying Dastards Away from Vegetables and Flowers in Daylight

If they eat more of your vegetables than you do, try aluminum foil. It's especially good as a deterrent for flying insects who invade in the daylight. They will not land in an area covered with foil, because the sun's ultraviolet rays are reflected by the foil, and that disturbs them. The foil will give protection to about 3 feet above ground level. Use heavy-duty foil. It usually comes 18 inches wide.

If you get it in bolts of 100 feet, two of them will cover a 10 x 10-foot unplanted plot. Roll out the foil and then either cover the edges with soil or hold them in place with stones or bricks.

If you're using foil on an established garden, you'll have to cut to size and fit accordingly. The foil will also hold the moisture in the ground and increase the available light and temperature. During the early stages of growth, your plants will develop more rapidly than usual. Truck farmers have been using foil with success for more than twenty years. It's certainly worth a try.

Neat Way to Find Insects

Lots of insects hide under leaves where you can't see them easily. Outsmart them with my secret. Take a regular spatula or pancake turner and glue a mirror to it. With this king-sized version of your dentist's mirror, you'll never have to stand on your head to find those monsters lurking under the leaves.

Grasshopper Protection

Grasshoppers are dumb but destructive dastards. Before they start to eat your tiny seedlings, lay a piece of cheesecloth over the seedlings. As they grow, they'll hold up the cloth, but the grasshoppers will be too dumb to get under it.

How to Keep Worms Out of Cauliflower

When heads are still small—1 to 2 inches in diameter—put each one in a nylon stocking and tie it below the head. When the heads get too big, remove the stocking.

How to Be Unfriendly to a Cucumber Beetle

These little demons eat more than cukes. They eat bean and pea plants, in addition to watermelon, gourd, squash, pumpkin, muskmelon and cantaloupe plants. Try filling a small saucer or lid of a jar with mothballs and setting it out near your plants—even before germination. The beetles hate the odor.

Why It's Difficult to Find Cutworms, and
How to Foil Them

You can always find their damage, but not them. Like all evil characters, they work at night and hide by day under loose earth or beneath stones curled up head-to-tail. Handpicking them is effective but tedious. The chemicals that really gave them a KO punch are now illegal. A good way to foil them is to place a 4-inch cardboard collar around each young plant and bury it about an inch deep in the soil. Or place a 5 x 8-inch filing card around each seedling like a box.

Another Way to Fool Cutworms—Some of Them

Here's a secret that often foils cutworms around tomatoes and peppers. Push a straight stick into the ground right up against your pepper and tomato plants when you're planting them. Be sure the stick touches the stem of the plant and rises about 2 inches above the ground. This usually works remarkably well, because the stick prevents the cutworm from wrapping its saw-toothed body around a young plant stem to squeeze it to death. Good always triumphs over evil.

Or Try This Way

Cutworms can be mightily discouraged by wrapping a 2-inch piece of brown paper around the stem of the cabbage seedling before planting.

Wood Ashes for Cutworms

Wood ashes are so useful not only as a nutrient for your soil, but as a deterrent to some insects like cutworms and some animals like deer and rabbits. Save the ashes from every fire you have; they're precious. When you use them to deter cutworms, make a circle of wood ashes around the plant you want to protect. The cutworms won't cross the ring. Neither will the animals—usually.

More Uses for Wood Ashes

Spread wood ashes around the base of cauliflower and onion plants for maggot control and around cabbage to repel snails or slugs. Wood ashes are also known to guard against red spiders and bean beetles, prevent scab on beets and turnips, and keep aphids off peas and lettuce. All this and they fertilize the soil, too. That's why I repeat—don't ever throw away even a thimbleful of wood ashes.

More More More Uses for Wood Ashes

If you want to control tree borers, mix wood ashes with enough water to make a paste and spread it on tree trunks. For controlling cucumber beetles, make a spray by mixing ½ cup of wood ashes and ½ cup of hydrated lime in 2 gallons of water. Spray on both sides of the cucumber plant leaves. Wear gloves when handling the lime.

Deter Cabbage Worms

Here's a goody. Use geranium trimmings to keep cabbage worms away. They evidently don't like the odor. Take about a 3-inch-long piece of geranium and set it on the head of the cabbage, stem down, with the lower leaves lying as flat as possible on the cabbage. If the cabbage is large, use several pieces of geranium.

Or, Do It the Kosher Way

At the first sight of a cabbage worm, sprinkle coarse kosher salt into the outer leaves of your cabbage. It takes about three applications, because those worms are tenacious little beasts. The outer leaves may become dry from the salt, but it won't affect the rest of the head.

More on Wildlife Under Cabbage Leaves

There are hardly any sprays you can use on cabbage without contaminating it. However, if you proceed with caution, you can spray cabbage with an ounce of salt dissolved in a gallon of water. You've got to be careful with this spray—make sure it doesn't get into the soil. Spread newspaper around the plant while spraying, and keep it there until the spray dries.

How to Deter Gourd Borers

These dastards are real stinkers. They wait until your gourds are almost ready for picking and then wham, bam, dam. I have heard that radish seeds deter borers, so plant them in the same hill with the gourds. If you allow your gourds to run on the ground, sow radish seeds along their paths. Leave the radishes in the ground and allow them to go to seed.

Be an Instant Garden Expert

Did you know that slugs are both male and female? First, the male sexual organs develop and eventually degenerate. Then the female organs develop and take over completely. Slugs can also fertilize their own eggs, and when two slugs mate, both will lay fertile eggs. So kill the little dastards every time you see one, or we'll be up to our you-know-whats in slugs.

Sourdough for Slugs

Beer is just too good to waste on slugs. These terribly slimy pests really go for beer—they will literally drown themselves in it. But what a waste! Actually, it's the smell of the yeast they like. Well, fool them. Sourdough mix also has a strong odor of yeast. Put some dough mix in whatever trap you're using to catch them.

Another Slug Killer

Water. Boiling water. It'll kill the slugs and their eggs or larvae. The only trouble is that you've got to know pretty much where the slugs are. If you think you do, go out in the early morning with a kettle of boiling water and pour it on the area where you believe them to be. The ground is cool in the morning, and the hot water won't hurt the roots of any nearby plants.

And Still Another Slug and Snail Killer

Try 3 tablespoons of Epsom salts to 1 gallon of water. Pour it over those areas where you think the slugs are hiding out.

How to Get Rid of Codling Moths

I have an apple-growing friend who swears by this method. If you're pestered by codling moths, the orchard man's enemy, try it. As soon as you see a moth, place the biggest tub of water you can find under or near your apple tree. Over the tub, suspend a 60- or 75-watt bulb. The moths will be attracted to the light and will then fall into the water.

How to Get Rid of Squash Borers

If you grow squash, save the ashes from all ashtrays. Sprinkle them around your squash plants and you'll deter squash borers. If it doesn't work, all you've done is made a silly ash of yourself.

Deter the Potato Bug

Plant horseradish at the corners of your potato garden.

Beat Japanese Beetles at Their Own Game

Japanese beetles love to eat grapes. The secret is to attract them with grape juice and this sneaky trap. Take a pail with a handle and wire a small can to it so the can is smack in the middle of the pail. Fill the can about three-quarters full with grape juice, and, for good measure, toss in a few grapes. Now fill the pail with water, but only

to the bottom of your can of grape juice. Put the contraption on top of your grape arbor or somewhere high near the grapevine. The beetles will be attracted by the grape aroma and head for it. But they are clumsy and will usually miss the small can and fall into the pail of water and drown. Tricky, aren't we?

More Uses for Garlic

I'm beginning to believe that garlic is probably the most useful of all plants. Garlic deters many insects, and it has a controlling effect on downy mildew, tomato blight and bacterial bean blight. All you have to do is grow it near many of your precious flowers and vegetables. The garlic does the rest. Throughout history, garlic has also been known to prevent disease. Dioscorides, the Greek physician who traveled with second-century Roman legions, specified garlic for intestinal disorders. Doctors today, too, respect it for its many useful properties. To give you an idea how fast garlic can travel through your body, rub some on the bottom of your feet some night. By morning you'll smell it on your breath. You'd better sleep alone if you try it.

More Uses for Herbs Besides Eating

Mint is very helpful in discouraging insects around cabbage and broccoli. Basil, when put in a sunny window, will keep the flies away. Chives and garlic are a great help around grapevines, fruit trees, raspberries and roses. Garlic also keeps cats out of the rose beds.

Another Great Spray for Aphids, Red Spider and
Control of Club Root

It's practically oxalic acid, and you brew it yourself. Steep 1½ pounds of rhubarb leaves in a gallon of water for 24 hours and then strain. Besides using it as a spray, pour it in the planting holes of cabbages and other members of the cabbage family—Brussels sprouts, broccoli, cauliflower, etc. It will also help control club root. Club root, in case you didn't know, is the result of roots becoming a mass of club-shaped swellings. When the swellings occur, cabbages and related vegetables won't develop firm heads, their growth will be stunted, and they will eventually turn yellow.

Don't make your garden too big if your wife tires easily.

JACQUES PIEROT III

Chapter Six

Houseplant Secrets

HOW TO CARE FOR THE
MOST PERFECT GUESTS
YOU'LL EVER HAVE

PLAYING MOTHER NATURE INDOORS

How to Sterilize Soil the Noseproof Way

It's always best to germinate seeds and grow houseplants in sterilized soil, so if you don't buy it, you've got to sterilize soil yourself. The smell is ghastly, I warn you. The way to do it is to moisten it and bake it in a 200° oven for 2 hours, or to cook it in a pressure cooker for 20 minutes at 15 pounds pressure. Now, do it this way. When you're having an outdoor barbecue, put in an extra amount of coals; then, after all the cooking is done, set your covered pan of soil on the dying coals. By the time the coals have died, the soil should be sterilized. Easy, neat and—best of all—smellproof.

How to Make Instant Soil in an Apartment

Instead of carting soil into your apartment from the country or buying it prepackaged, try this growing mixture. You'll find it's far more satisfactory for an apartment and—even more important—good for your plants.

To make two bushels of instant apartment soil, use:

1 bushel sphagnum moss
½ bushel vermiculite
½ bushel perlite
10 tablespoons ground limestone
5 tablespoons superphosphate (20%)
2 tablespoons potassium nitrate (14-0-44)
1 level teaspoon chelated iron

Mix everything together and then add *one* of the following plant foods. Repeat, add only *one* of the following plant foods:

2.3 ounces Scotts (23-7-7)
3.8 ounces Peters (14-7-7)
1.5 ounces Nitroform, Uramite or Borden's 38

How to Make Potting Soil Acid

If you don't want to buy a special fertilizer just for plants that like an acid soil, use aluminum sulfate. You can buy it at most garden stores or nurseries. Mix about ½ teaspoon into the soil of a

4-inch pot. With that easy formula you don't have to be an Einstein to figure out how much you need for other-sized pots.

A Compost Pile in Your Kitchen

You've certainly heard of the wondrous things compost does for your soil. But suppose you live in an apartment house and have no place for one? Ah—but you do. You can make your own compost pile in a window box and give all its goodies to your houseplants. You'll have the same stuff people with a regular compost heap use on their gardens. Here's how. Get some regular soil from a garden—sterilized soil from the florist's or a nursery may not work. You only need a layer of it about an inch high to line your window box. Then, as you get them, add coffee grounds, vegetable peelings, and eggshells. Stir it all once in a while and add water once in a while, but not much. Too much water will give it an odor. If you have a dog or cat, his contribution can be used, too, but cover it with soil or you'll regret it. The wonders of Nature will happen before your very eyes. The bacteria in the soil will break down everything you put into your "heap," and soon you'll be able to tell how long the peelings and everything else you dump into it will take to disappear and turn into humus. Orange peels, for instance, take longer than carrot peels, but none take too long. And if you water sparingly, there is no unpleasant odor. The odor is like that of a lush jungle rain forest.

Save Your Eggshells for Houseplants

Eggshells will give your houseplants all kinds of nutrients. They are a good source of nitrogen, phosphoric acid and calcium; they will also contribute considerable lime to your soil if added frequently. Mix the eggshells directly into your potting soil.

Geritol for Tired Plants

Would you believe it—Geritol for an ailing plant? I saw the miracle, or so it seemed. A friend had a large philodendron that had lost its foliage. In desperation, and with great humor, he poured Geritol onto his plant regularly for three months. At the end of the first month new leaves began to appear. Today it is one of his most beautiful plants. The formula he found best is 1 tablespoon every other day. Maybe it was the constant attention and not the Geritol that made the difference. But whatever it was—it worked.

KEEPING THEM ALIVE—WITH AND WITHOUT WATER

Overwatering vs. Too Much Watering

Don't be confused—there is a difference. Overwatering means watering *too often*. Too much means giving your plants too much water at any one time. Whenever directions caution you not to overwater, leave the plant alone until it is dry to the touch. Then give it a lot of water. If your pot has proper drainage, the excess water will drain away quickly.

How to Make Self-Watering Pots

Here's a way to make a pot water itself for about two weeks. It will feed itself, too, if you put soluble fertilizer in the water. I'll give you the general idea and you can improvise if need be. You'll need a plastic margarine tub and lid, or a plastic refrigerator or freezer container (you can buy them in all sizes). Next get some wicks, or some nylon cord such as a clothesline (#24 weight). Before you pot your plant, run the wick or cord halfway through the pot. Then put in about ½ inch of charcoal chips and fill the pot half full with potting soil. Lay the cord across the soil. Add more soil and then the plant. Next, make two holes in the lid of the plastic container, a larger one at the side for filling purposes and a smaller one at the center for the wick. Set your plant on top of the lidded plastic tub. The wick will now work its magic, gently watering your plant as needed until the water supply is gone.

A Crazy Way to Tell if Your Plant Needs Watering

If your plant is in a clay pot, you can tell when it needs watering by snapping the pot with your fingernail. If it makes a thud, it has enough water. If you get a ringing sound, it needs water.

Or—Use a Finger Test for Watering

Even if you were blindfolded, you could tell with the finger test whether your plants needed watering. Scratch the soil lightly, about ⅛ inch below the surface. Now put that same finger to your cheek. If it feels cool, your plant does not need watering. If it doesn't, get going.

Easy Way to Water and Sun Indoor Plants

Put them on a lazy Susan—the plastic turntables made for kitchen shelves. A 20-inch one will hold a number of small pots, and you can easily rotate it for sun, watering and grooming. You should, however, put a layer of pebbles on the turntable before you set the plants out. Water spills will disappear and keep everything very tidy.

Found—A Use for Old Aquarium Water

This is a goody. Do you know that the ammonia wastes from fish are a good source of nitrogen? If you have an aquarium, use the old water each week on your plants, especially the leafy plants.

Best Kind of Water for Ferns and African Violets

Both plants object to chlorine in water, so pamper them by letting the water you use on them stand overnight in an open container. Or you can always boil the water, but that's the hard way.

How to Water a Hanging Basket Without
Breaking Your Neck

Here's a neat secret; after you learn it you'll wonder why you never thought of it. Instead of standing on a chair or ladder to water baskets, or reaching up until your arms hurt, simply poke a pinhole (and a small pinhole at that—more a pinprick) in the bottom of a small plastic bottle or cup. Fill it with water and place it in the middle of your basket. This will allow the water to seep out slowly into the soil rather than onto you or the carpet.

How to Stop Dripping Baskets

Nothing is more aggravating than to water a hanging basket, only to have it drip all over the floor or carpet. Here's my secret for preventing this. Slip a plastic shower cap over the bottom of the basket until the watering is done.

How You Can Water Your Plants
Even Though You're Not There

If you're going on vacation and can't find a plant sitter, do this. Water each plant thoroughly and then cover completely with a clear plastic bag such as those you get from the cleaner. Place it in a cool location out of direct sunlight. Plants will last like this for 2 to 3 weeks.

If your plants are in porous containers such as clay pots, stand them on bricks in a watertight container such as a sink or bathtub. Bring the water level up to the tops of the bricks. This system will work well for plants too large to fit in the plastic bags. It should also take care of your plants for about three weeks.

Another Way to Keep Plants Moist While
You're on Vacation

The trick is to figure out which way is more suitable for your kind of plants. One lady I know waters her plants thoroughly, then completely covers their containers with very wet towels, which she then covers with plastic wrap.

Plants for Dry Skin

If you have dry skin, humidity in your rooms will help it. If the room you are in more often than any other during the day is very dry, make it humid by keeping plants in it. You'll help your skin (and your plants) even more if the plants and their saucers are kept on a tray of pebbles filled with water.

How to Bathe Your Plants

Houseplants need a bath now and then, just as thee and me. (The only exceptions are those with hairy-surfaced leaves, such as African violets and some begonias.) Use warm soapy water—and be sure you use real soap. Wash all leaves, stems and buds with a soft sponge, holding your hand under each individual leaf so you'll be sure to clean both sides. Rinse with clear water, shake and allow to dry overnight in the sink or on a newspaper. If done once every month, this will remove dirt, insects and their eggs and bring out the natural shine of the foliage.

LITTLE-KNOWN FACTS ABOUT
WELL-KNOWN PLANTS

Success (at Last) with Miniature Roses

Miniature roses are lovely little plants and, though small, are very hardy in the garden. The problem so many people have with them is growing them indoors. The reason is usually insufficient sunlight and humidity. Indoors they should be grown in full sunlight (or not at all), and the pots should be put in a tray filled with pebbles or sand which is kept wet all the time. They can also be grown under a plant light kept on for 18 hours daily and positioned only an inch or two above the plant. Yet even with these two essentials, sunlight and humidity, there's another and most important secret to growing miniature roses successfully. This secret I learned from the famous Star Rose Nursery in Pennsylvania. After the roses have given you gorgeous bloom all winter and spring, give them an 8-week rest during June and July in the vegetable compartment of your refrigerator, the hydrator. After all, if they were growing outdoors, they'd have that rest in the winter. After the rest period, prune plants back to about 3 inches, stand back and watch 'em grow!

What You Should Know About Gloxinia

Gloxinia fans will argue that there's a lot more to know about their favorite plant than the following (and there is), but these are the basics—enough information to assure you some lovely blooms. Gloxinia gets its large lush flowers from plenty of light—from 14 to 16 hours a day—and plenty of humidity. After it blooms, allow the plant to go dormant by decreasing the water until all the foliage has died. Let the tuber rest without water for from 6 to 10 weeks. When you see new growth appear, then you start watering again. It will take 4 to 5 months to get blooms, and it's worth every minute of it.

What You Should Know About Columnea

First, you ought to know about this lovely plant, if you don't already. It belongs to the same family as the African violet. Grown in a hanging basket, it makes one of the most attractive, really handsome indoor vines there is, with its brilliant scarlet, carmine or yellow flowers. *Columnea gloriosa,* for example, has large vividly yellow and scarlet tubular flowers and is quite a sight. You can grow columnea in your sunniest window or under 40-watt fluorescent lights for 12 to 14 hours daily. They are tropical plants and need a humid atmosphere. In the summer keep them away from the fiercest rays of the sun.

How to Stop Violet Leaves from Rotting

Violet leaves that touch the edges of their pots have a tendency to rot. You can prevent this by dipping the rims of the violet pots in hot wax. Melt your old candles or use paraffin.

How to Get More Flowers from Your African Violets

If you've got a healthy plant and few flowers, the trouble may be that the water you use on them is alkaline. Try rainwater or distilled water or spring water. Or once a month, put vinegar in the water you give the violets, a teaspoon to a quart of water. I bet it'll help.

Cleaning African Violets

Leaves need to be cleaned occasionally. The easiest way is to brush a pipe cleaner against the grain of the leaf.

"Variegating" Variegated Violets

Many growers of African violets with variegated foliage feel that lime helps to hold the variegation. They mix it into the soil or add it to the water. You can do the same, but never do it at the same time as you're fertilizing, because it can cause loss of nitrogen. Use a pinch of hydrated lime.

Be an Instant Garden Expert

Did you know that the African violet is not a violet, but it does come from Africa? Its botanical name is *Saintpaulia,* after the Baron von Saintpaul who was a commissioner in Africa. He found this African beauty and sent it home to Germany in 1892.

Jade Plants

So many people who own these attractive succulents overwater them. Because they are succulents, their fat, fleshy leaves are able to store water for long periods of time. So remember that from September to April, jade plants need not be watered more than once a month.

Lily-of-the-Valley

Lily-of-the-valley, that heavenly scented spring beauty, has a very accurate schedule. If you want to force it so you'll get blooms right smack at Christmas, plant the pips on December third. Lily-of-the-valley takes exactly 21 days after planting to bloom.

Stout's Way with Gardenias

If you don't know who Ruth Stout is, it's time you learned. She's practically the mother of organic gardening and a storehouse of garden knowledge. She says the reason most people have trouble grow-ing a gardenia indoors is that they give it too much sun and too little humidity. When gardenia buds turn brown and drop off, it's because there's insufficient humidity in the air. Madame Stout advises keeping the plant in strong light only and placing the pot in a saucer of water which is always kept filled. As the water evaporates, it rises and bathes the gardenia with the moisture the plant craves. I personally prefer to place water in a small pie pan or bowl on *top* of the soil. If you don't like to look at pans or bowls on top of the gardenia soil, cover the sur-face with sheet sphagnum moss.

Another Gardenia Secret

If the buds still drop even after you provide more humidity, get out the lifesaving cleaner's plastic bag. Completely cover the gardenia plant with the bag and keep it there. Take it off only when you have guests. It will also help if you put a little vinegar in the water when watering. A half-teaspoon of vinegar to a quart of water will do it. Or if you've got fertilizer for acid-loving plants, use it.

What You Should Know About Wax Begonias

They need lots of morning sun and not too much water. This is the secret to growing this very attractive houseplant. People forget that wax begonias are succulent and store water in their stems and leaves for use in periods of dryness. Too much water will make the plant rot. So watch it with the H_2O.

Rex Begonias

I've always considered this plant the king of houseplants. It sort of lives up to its name, too. It's very difficult to grow from seed and, when grown, very temperamental and demanding. It demands warmth, good bright light (not strong sun but strong light) and moderately moist soil. Too many rex begonias are killed with too much water. If its leaf edges turn brown, it means the plant needs more humidity, not more watering.

How to Get Bromeliads to Flower

Some bromeliad plants never flower because there is not enough ethylene gas in the air. Bromeliads are part of the pineapple family and include such lovely plants as aechmea, billbergia, crypt-anthus, nidularium, tillandsia and vriesia. They can be made to bloom very easily with an apple, of all things. Apples give off ethylene gas, so the secret is to stick an apple in a plastic bag along with your bromeliad, pot and all. Leave it for three or four days and then remove bag and apple. In a couple of months your bromeliad will begin to bloom.

Feed Your Bromeliad Banana Peels

You read it correctly. Feed your bromeliads with one or two ½-inch pieces of banana peel by dropping them into the overlapping leaves, which become the watering "tank" of a bromeliad. Change the supply every week. You can also use a diluted fish emulsion (never use chemical fertilizers on bromeliads), but it's better to stick to the banana peels if your bromeliad is near you during day or night. The fish emulsion has, not surprisingly, a terrible, lingering dead fish odor.

How to Keep "Foliageless" Plants Alive

Just because a plant has lost its foliage doesn't necessarily mean it is on its last legs. Keep it drier than usual, and, with a little luck, new foliage will begin to develop. Then start watering it.

What to Do When You Have More Leaves than Flowers

Lush foliage in a flowering plant means you've got too much nitrogen in the soil. Use a fertilizer low in nitrogen, such as a 7-6-10 formula. Forget not: the lower the first number of any fertilizer formula, the lower the nitrogen content.

How to Get Avocados from an Avocado Houseplant

If you've ever grown this beautiful foliage plant, you know it doesn't bear fruit. Like everything else, it takes two to tango. If you have your heart set on fruit, then grow two different avocado varieties so that the flowers can be fertilized. Not by bees, but by you. Cross-fertilize with a Q-tip.

Instant Garlic

Grow a "hint" of garlic. Stick toothpicks into the sides of a garlic clove. Suspend it in a glass of water, with the root end of the bud touching the water. In a few days green shoots will begin to sprout. Use the shoots in a salad for a very mild garlic flavor.

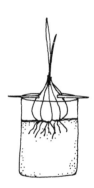

Watercress on Your Windowsill

You can grow it there easily the year round just so long as you keep it forever damp. Its soil should have a lot of compost or peat moss in it, as well as a number of pieces of broken clay pots in the bottom of the container. The clay will give you good drainage and a bonus—it gives off lime, and lime is what watercress likes. If you're going to grow it from seed, presoak the seed for 18 to 24 hours for faster germination.

An easier way is to buy a bunch of fresh watercress at the supermarket, strip the bottom leaves off, and put the watercress in rainwater or water without chemicals. Keep the cuttings in sunlight or very bright light, and change the water every day. You'll get roots in about 2 to 4 days. When they are about 2 inches long, plant. Keep the soil wet at all times, and keep the container in which your watercress is growing in a saucer filled with water.

What to Grow in Water and Some Secrets on How

Mighty pretty specimens can be grown in water in your home. Plants grown in water will do well if you don't try to transplant them to soil after they have rooted. That usually spells diaster. Try these in water: ivy, dieffenbachia, Chinese evergreen, dracaena, umbrella palm, variegated wandering Jew, Hawaiian ti, tree fern, arrowhead, coleus and pachysandra. Of the entire list, I can only recommend planting pachysandra in soil after it has been rooted in water. Once in soil, it must be watered continually until it takes hold.

Before you put your plants in water, let the water stand at least 24 hours in a wide container so that the chlorine (if it isn't well water) will evaporate. Always use water at room temperature. Check the pH of your water with litmus paper. If it is too alkaline, add a few drops of white vinegar. If it is too acid, add a little baking soda. When the pH is right, add a few pieces of charcoal to keep the water sweet. If you don't have an outdoor barbecue, you can pick up small quantities of charcoal sold for pet birds in the supermarket, the pet shop, or the five-and-ten. Feed plants about once a month, using a soluble plant food in either powder or tablet form at half the recommended strength.

Secrets About Poinsettia

When buying this "short day" plant (so called because it needs more darkness than light to flower), pick a plant with green foliage all the way down the stem. If the lower leaves are gone, chances are that the root system is not all it should be. When you're transporting a poinsettia, don't expose it to a temperature below 50° or the leaves will drop. Once home, water it until the excess drains out of the bottom onto a saucer. Fertilize well, since it probably hasn't been fed for some time. Keep the plant away from drafts and hot radiators, in a spot where it will receive at least 6 hours of sunlight a day. With luck, your new plant should put on a good show for you for the next three or four months.

In June cut the stems very short—all the way back to an inch above the crotch of each stem. That way you'll have twice as many blooms the following year. Summer them outdoors in full sun and fertilize twice a month.

In September or October (before frost), bring your plant back indoors and put it in an absolutely dark closet from six o'clock in the evening to eight the next morning. The ideal temperature for that absolutely dark closet (and no peeking) is about 60°. Make sure there is no light coming from under the door. After a month or six weeks of this dark treatment, put it in a bright window, and at about Christmas you should once again have magnificent flowers.

If You Don't Have a Closet

Okay, you know your poinsettia needs six weeks of long nights in total darkness, but you haven't any room to spare in your closets. Don't despair. Go to your local appliance store and wheedle a large cardboard box—don't bother with the supermarket boxes; they are usually not large enough to cover a poinsettia that has grown outdoors all summer. Cover the plant with the box at 6 P.M. and uncover it again in the morning.

LET THERE BE LIGHT

Shedding Some Light on African Violets

They need 14 to 16 hours of light daily during the dark days of winter. In the summer, 10 to 12 hours daily. If the leaves seem to be bunching up, it means the violets need more fertilizer or they are getting too much light. Cyclamen mites also will cause the violet crowns to bunch up, but then the leaves usually grow a dull green.

How to Tell if Your African Violet Has Enough Light

There is a way to tell if your plant is getting enough light. If it is, the leaves will lie parallel to the table. In other words, absolutely flat. If the leaves turn upward, the plant is not getting enough light. On the other hand, if the leaves turn downward, there is too much light. Usually if the top of your plant is about 6 to 8 inches from the artificial light, you have nothing to worry about.

How to Tell if You've Got Enough Light on Your Plants

Light is measured by footcandles. If you want to splurge, you can buy yourself a footcandle meter. It costs under $25. You can also use a regular photographic light meter from your camera. Set the ASA exposure index to 75, the lens opening to f/8. Use an exposure time of one-sixtieth of a second. This will give you the equivalent of 1,000 footcandles. When you double the ASA index of the exposure time, or use one f-stop larger, you get 500 footcandles. One f-stop less, or half the ASA index, gives you 2,000 footcandles.

An aspidistra needs very little light; it will grow in about 50 footcandles. German ivy requires from 450 to 650 footcandles. Christmas cherry or tuberous begonia needs at least 1,000 footcandles. Illuminating—yes?

Another Way to Tell if Your Plant Has Enough Light

If the light is strong enough to read by or to do fine needle-work comfortably, there is enough light for all but sun-loving plants.

Get Greener Plants Indoors

Did you know that fluorescent lamps produce a deeper green on plant foliage than ordinary incandescent house bulbs? But—and here's the big secret—incandescent bulbs will give you more flowers.

A Secret for Growing Under Artificial Light

Artificial light sops up much of the humidity plants need in order to grow. Instead of putting just one plant under a light, put as many as you can fit under the light. That will leave less soil exposed to air. If you insist on having only one plant under the light, place the pot in a larger pot and put sphagnum moss in the bottom of the larger pot. Keep the moss wet—really wet—and hold onto that humidity.

Increase Windowsill Light Even on Rainy Days

If you're growing plants on the windowsill, line it with foil or mirrors. Both will not only reflect more light, but protect your sills. If you're growing vegetables on the sill, the extra light and warmth will produce a faster and higher yield.

How to Get More Light in Your Indoor Garden Without Electricity

If your garden is in your basement or even in a closet and all the light it gets is artificial light, here's how to increase it without paying a cent extra for electricity. Paint the walls and ceiling white. If the area is small, line the walls with aluminum foil. It will reflect the light marvelously. Also put a mirror at the end of a growing section. The mirror will not only reflect the light, but will also make your garden look twice as big as it is.

Another Way to Get More Light Without Electricity

Double the light for your potted plants by using aluminum pie plates as saucers. They'll help deflect the light to the plants' lower leaves.

Starting Plants Indoors Without Much Window Space

If you don't have enough window space to plant all the seeds you want, don't give up. Push a card table or any table to the window, get yourself a cardboard carton (your supermarket will give you all you want), and make a three-sided wall with the carton. Tack aluminum foil to the inside of the box—the three sides and the bottom. Plant your seeds in containers and put them inside the box. When they germinate they will get all the light they need, because the foil will reflect the sun's rays from every direction. What's more, your containers will not have to be constantly turned to face the light. This is a marvelous secret if you live in an apartment with only a little window space.

Brighten Your Darkest Corner with a Plant

The best plants for dark corners are Chinese evergreen (*Aglaonema*), dwarf palm (*Chamaedorea elegans*), *Dracaena fragrans* and pothos.

What to Do When It's Impossible to Give Plants Much Light

I'm against growing plants under those circumstances, but if you must, water them only enough to prevent wilting. Cut the fertilizer in half. Keep air temperature as cool as you can. And pray.

Why Leaves Turn White

Plant leaves will often turn white in a sunny area. The reason, madam or sir, is that your plant is getting a suntan. Take it out of the sun for a while and then bring it back gradually, but don't ever give it as much sun as it had been getting.

Make Yourself an Indoor Hanging Garden

Even the smallest room can be turned into something spectacular and it won't cost much. Here's a plan for an 8 x 10 room. Use more or less material, depending on the size of your room. Install three 8-foot fluorescent cool white lights on the ceiling. Below them, hang a trellis made of 1-inch laths spaced to create a grid of 12-inch squares below the ceiling. Hang your baskets from the trellis. The result is simply fabulous.

MINI-GREENHOUSE. MINI-TERRARIUMS. MINI-EXPENSE

Your Very Own Plant Hospital, Nursing Home and Exclusive Greenhouse

How would you like all that in your own home? You've got it and you didn't even know it. It all comes from plastic bags—cleaner's bags, bread bags, vegetable bags, sandwich bags—in fact, any plastic bag you can see through. Never throw one away because you will find hundreds of uses for them. For example, creating your own hospital. A big beautiful houseplant is very sick, infected with mites. What to do besides giving up and tossing the plant in the garbage can? You put it in the "hospital" by covering it with a cleaner's plastic bag. Put a pest strip inside the bag. Make sure the entire plant is under the bag. In a couple of days remove the plant from its hospital. You'll find it in very good health and its ailment gone. Plastic bags placed loosely over a plant or cuttings are also a marvelous way to provide steady humidity in a dry room.

As stated elsewhere in this book, bags placed over plants while you're on vacation will prevent moisture evaporation. Another use for plastic bags is in transporting plants during cold weather. I've gone to many a flower show in the East with my treasures insulated from the frigid winds, each in its own plastic bag.

How to Make a Greenhouse for Miniature Orchids That Costs Peanuts

When space is limited and you'd like to grow orchids, here's a great compromise—miniature orchids in their own miniature green-house. It's so simple to make. Place a wire rack on the bottom of a

12 x 12-inch dishpan. It will hold nine or more of the 2- or 3-inch pots in which you will grow the miniature orchids. Keep the bottom of the dishpan filled with water; the rack will keep the orchid pots above the water. If you place the dishpan inside a large plastic bag, the water will provide all the humidity the orchids need. The top of the bag can

be sealed at night and slipped down around the sides of the pan during the day. The result is a compact, humid greenhouse at night, and one that gets circulating fresh air all day. Fresh air is absolutely essential for orchids. Perfect. And perfectly cheap.

Another Miniature Greenhouse Idea

You can also make a greenhouse out of a plastic bread box or a sweater box with a clear top. Both will hold a number of small pots in the same climate they could get in a real greenhouse. Put gravel on the bottom of the box to keep the pots above any water that might collect there. Don't forget to lift the top of the "greenhouse" if the air in it becomes too humid.

Mini-Terrariums

For decoration, for cuttings, for any plant that needs high humidity, a no-expense mini-terrarium can be made from two plastic cold-drink glasses. For the bottom, use the wide-mouthed ones (the

kind old-fashioneds are served in). For the top, use a standard-size water glass. When you invert the standard-size glass, you'll find it fits snugly into the top of the old-fashioned glass. For ventilation, use a thick needle (heated) to burn several holes in the bottom of the upper glass.

Make Your Own Terrarium

The odder the shape, the more interesting the terrarium. An old Silex coffeemaker without the handle makes an interesting one. Or try the more interesting—and more difficult—mustard jars, laboratory flasks, apple cider jugs, and applesauce jars. Anybody can use an old fish tank for a terrarium. You be different. If you use your noggin, you'll find one that will suit your life-style. For example, a new mother can make a terrarium in a baby bottle by placing tiny rooted cuttings around a lamb or other animal figurines. This, by the way, makes a charming maternity gift.

Tools for Your Terrarium

You can make most of them yourself. Wire a spoon to the end of a dowel and you'll have a handy shovel for digging. Place a funnel on a small piece of surgical or plastic hose and you'll have a handy gadget for watering and for spreading charcoal dust. If you want something for removing condensation from the sides of your terrarium, tie a soft cloth around some heavy but flexible wire.

Make Your Own Funnel

If you need a funnel for your terrarium, make one. Roll one out of the heaviest paper you have in the house and staple the sides together.

Another Tool for the Terrarium

An ear syringe with a length of plastic tubing attached to it will shoot the water into your terrarium just where you want it.

More Handmade Tools for Terrariums

A tweezer is a must for a terrarium, and here's a way to make a long one. Get an 18-inch bamboo stake and split it almost to the end. Leave about 2 inches, and tie those 2 inches with a rubber band to prevent further splitting. Insert a small wooden peg in the center to keep the tweezer opened, and then wrap another rubber band around the tweezer where the peg is. Sounds slightly complicated, but it does work.

Another Handy Tool for Your Terrarium

You know those X-acto blades the kids use for cutting model airplanes? They make ideal tools for pruning plants in a terrarium. Wire or glue the blade onto the end of a chopstick or a plant stake for a miniature saw. You can buy the blades at hobby shops.

FROM THE NEVER-FORGET-IT DEPARTMENT

What Not to Do with Brand-New Store-Bought or Gift Plants

Don't—repeat, *don't*—put them with your other plants immediately. Keep them away from other plants for at least a month, just in case they are infected with whiteflies, mites, mealybugs or any other of the little dastards that can ruin an entire plant collection. Of course, I've got to be honest. I do not do this. I stick the new plant with the old established plants, often to my sorrow. So, do as I say, not as I do.

How to Revive Plants After Repotting

Plants often wilt after repotting, but don't panic. Spray the leaves with lukewarm water; then put pot and all into a large clear plastic bag and tie it closed. If you don't have a bag, make one out of the plastic "bags" you get from the cleaner's. In a day or two your plant will revive. Don't leave your plant under the plastic greenhouse for more than two days or mildew may form.

Glossier Leaves Free of Charge

You don't need to use cooking oil, mayonnaise or store-bought "shine" preparations to get rhododendron and other broad-leaved evergreens shiny. Wash them with warm soapy water, rinse and then rub them with waxed paper.

How to Clean Hairy-Leaved Plants

Use a soft sable paintbrush. Support the back of the leaf with your free hand. If you don't have a brush handy, a Q-tip works quite well.

When Plant Containers Don't Have Holes for Drainage

Here's a trick that will allow you to use any container you want to hold a favorite plant, even though it doesn't have drainage holes. Simply place a good layer of supercoarse perlite or small pebbles on the bottom of your container. Stand several drinking straws upright in the container so they just touch the perlite or pebbles. Then fill in with soil and put in your plant, leaving the straws poking out above the soil. When the soil settles, cut the straws a bit above the soil surface, but be careful you don't plug them with soil. Don't overwater.

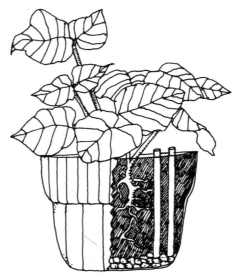

How to Handle Houseplants Outdoors

If you want to put your houseplants, pot and all, into the soil in the summer, put some wood ashes in the hole before you put in each pot. The ashes will keep insects from entering the pots through the drainholes.

Make Your Own Hanging Pot

You can turn an ordinary pot into a hanging pot by drilling three holes in the pot and threading wire or small chains through them. If the pot is plastic, heat a skewer or heavy nail and bore your holes with the heat. To drill clay pots, use a three-sixteenth-inch masonry drill. Choose light-colored red clay pots for drilling. The dark-colored red pots are fired harder and are more difficult to drill.

How to Sterilize Clay Pots

This is a must for good housekeeping. When you empty a clay pot, drop it into a tub or sink full of water and wash away the soil. Then sterilize the pot by immersing it in a solution of 1 part fluoride bleach to 9 parts water. Let it soak for at least 30 minutes. Do a lot of pots at a time, naturally.

Getting Rid of Gunk on Clay Pots

That white residue you often find on clay pots is not so difficult to get rid of, even though it is almost impossible to clean with soap and water or bleach. Simply soak the pots overnight in a tub of water to which you've added a quart of white vinegar. The next day, sponge off the white residue. Then soak the pots one more day in clear clean water. You can, of course, sterilize at the same time by adding bleach to the vinegar water.

Keeping Clay Saucers from Ruining Tables or Floors

Most of us put a clay saucer under our potted plants to prevent watermarks on the table, rug or floor. But a lot of us forget that clay saucers, like clay pots, absorb water and leave marks on the table, rug or floor. Avoid this by varnishing the saucer.

MORE FOR WHAT'S BUGGING YOU

Insect Control for Houseplants

Aphids, thrips and red spider can be washed off with luke-warm soapy water. Rinse the plant well and allow it to dry in a warm, shady location. Mealybugs can be totaled by simply touching them with a cotton swab dipped in alcohol.

Shoofly, Whitefly

The whitefly is the villain of the indoor plant world. There are some new good chemical sprays available, but if you're against their use, try Nature's way. Make successive plantings of Peruvian ground cherry (*Nicandra physalodes*), and keep a few plants continuously in bloom. Nicandra has delicate blue flowers and grows to a height of three feet. It's also called the shoofly plant. Some people believe that the flowers destroy whiteflies; others believe the plant's sap does. Who cares as long as the evil flies are destroyed?

More Shoofly, Whitefly

Here's another way to get rid of whitefly on your houseplants: hang an old-fashioned fly strip near the infected plants, and every once in a while shake the plants. The whiteflies will get caught in the fly paper. My favorite way to get rid of them, as I said earlier, is to put the entire plant in a plastic bag with a pest strip for a few days.

Get Rid of Ants with Eggshells

Would you believe ants can't stand the smell of eggshells? Save your eggshells, crush them, put them into a plastic berry basket, and set the basket where the ants are. They'll vanish like magic. The eggshells work equally well outdoors, too, but you won't need the basket. Just sprinkle them wherever needed. Two cautions. Don't use eggshells that have been boiled, for the smell is gone. Don't put the eggshells in cardboard berry baskets. The cardboard absorbs the eggshell odor. One bonus when you put eggshells on the ground—eventually they'll get into the soil, and the soil will absorb the lime from the shells.

Garlic for Roaches

Garlic is great for repelling so many insects that make our plants miserable outdoors, but did you know that you can repel roaches indoors with it? Peel a handful of garlic cloves, slitting them to let out some of that marvelous odor, and then put the cloves wherever you think the roaches are. Within two days the roaches should be gone. Renew the garlic every three to four weeks to keep the roaches away for good.

Another Way to Get Rid of Roaches

If you know where they are coming from, sprinkle Borax near the hole. They hate the odor. (But they hate garlic more.)

A SPRING GARDEN WITHOUT ANY
GARDEN OR ANY SPRING

Bulb Gardens for Apartment Balconies

All you need is an inexpensive styrofoam picnic hamper or ice chest to grow spring daffodils, tulips, hyacinths or whatever other spring bulbs strike your fancy. Drill holes in the chest for drainage and then fill with soil. In the fall, plant your bulbs, mulch lightly and place the chest against the wall of your balcony without the lid. If a cold snap should come in the spring after growth has started, simply put the lid on for protection.

Spring Bloom in Winter the Easy Way

Why bury your spring bulbs for winter forcing and then dig them out of frozen soil when there's an easier way? It's such a brilliant idea, I don't know why people didn't think of it before. Simply put your bulbs in their pots the usual way, and then place them in the vegetable drawer of your refrigerator for at least six weeks. Bring them into the light nine weeks before you want them to bloom. The first week you take them out of the refrigerator, put them in strong light, without any sun. After that, put them in full sun in the coolest spot in your house. *Voilà*—a beautiful spring garden any time of the year.

How to "Frame" a Tulip

Want a well-balanced tulip plant after forcing? Then study each tulip bulb. You'll find there's not only a top and bottom to a tulip bulb, but one flat side and one round side. When you're forcing bulbs, always be sure the flat side is facing the edge of the pot. This way the tulip will grow thick leaves, which will become its frame and make it pretty as a picture.

How to Force Lilies

No less an expert than Jan de Graaf, the famous lily hybridizer, shares his secret for forcing. Toward the end of October, place the lily bulbs in a plastic bag and store them in a refrigerator kept at between 34° and 40° for 6 weeks to 2 months. Then pot them and place them in a sunny spot. They'll flower in about 75 days. If you want lilies on Valentine's Day, pot them by November 24. If you plant them later in the spring, they do not take a full 75 days. For example, if you want them on Mother's Day, plant them on March 1.

For peat's sake, don't treat your soil like dirt.

ARLENE JACOBI

Chapter Seven

Winter Garden Secrets

DON'T BE ASLEEP
WHEN THEY ARE

PUTTING THE GARDEN TO BED—NO ROMANCE
BUT PLENTY OF ACTION

How to Get Rosebushes Ready for Winter

Don't feed your roses after August 5, or they won't be winter-hardy. Don't water heavily after September 15, and don't let the September blooms remain on the plants to set seed pods. They have a tendency to discourage new growth.

What to Do to Rosebushes After the First Frost

Prune back the tall growth of hybrid tea roses to three feet so there won't be any wind damage. (Save your heavy pruning for the spring.) When the ground is frozen, bring soil from another part of the garden and mound it up around your bush, about 6 to 10 inches above the soil level. Don't use soil from around the bush for your mounding; you could be robbing the rose's spreading roots of their needed winter protection.

Bring Nasturtium Vines Indoors

These vines are lovely in the house. They will grow for months in water if they are cut well before frost and then fed every week with a few drops of liquid fertilizer.

Fertilize Without Work

Don't pull out your annuals in the fall. Cut them at ground level so the soil will benefit from their decomposition.

Dahlias Live a Lot Longer Than You Think

Often an early frost will blacken the top portion of your dahlias. Leave them alone. Don't dig the roots at this time, because the dahlias will continue to bloom as long as a part of the plant is green.

How to Store Dahlia Tubers

Fill a box with garden soil and place the dahlia tubers on top of the soil. Cover them with about an inch of builders' sand. Store the box in a cool, dark spot. Water lightly after about three weeks and then only once a month until spring.

When to Winter Mulch

Do it *after* the ground is frozen solid. Remember, you're not covering your plants to keep out the cold, but to keep the cold in.

If you do it before the ground freezes, you make a nice cozy winter home for mice, with all the food they can eat—yours. Your bulbs and the roots of your plants.

What to Do with a Filled Strawberry Barrel
When Winter Comes

Strawberries usually survive in the winter, but sometimes the clay barrel doesn't. Here's how to save the barrel and at the same time provide pleasant, comfortable sleep for the strawberry plants.

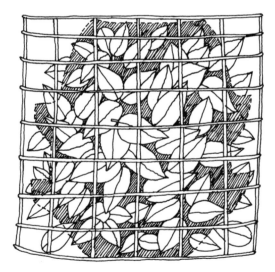

After the ground has frozen, make a cylinder around your barrel with chicken wire (as high as your barrel and several inches away from it). Connect the two ends with wire or string. Now fill the entire space between the wire and the barrel with leaves. You must do this after the ground has frozen, because, just as with the roses, the field mice will have a field day with a warm leaf home and delicious strawberry plants to tide them over the cold winter.

Protect Ground from Thawing and Heaving in Winter

Freezing doesn't hurt your plants, but the thawing of the frozen ground can cause the plants to heave out during a mild spell in the winter. Covering plants with branches can help prevent all that, but often there aren't enough branches available. There will be if you wait until the day after Christmas. Often, unsold Christmas trees can be had for the asking or taking. They make a great ground cover.

How to Outwit Field Mice During Winter

If you see any, chances are they are living under your rose mulch. Before you mulch your roses each winter, circle the plants with poison bait.

Don't Use Salt for Icy Pavement

Salt around or near ornamental plants can ruin them even though the ground is frozen. Use sand instead.

How to Handle Winter Sprays

When you winterproof certain plants to prevent moisture loss in the winter, spray only the topside of the leaves. This will allow the plant to breathe through the underside.

How to Be an Instant Garden Expert

Did you know that snow is one of the best insulators there is against cold? Think about it. An Eskimo makes his igloo of snow. A candle or two is all he needs to keep himself warm, thanks to the insulating qualities of the snow. That's why snow is so great for the life of our plants in the winter, in case you never thought about it.

When to Pick a Gourd

Gourds should be picked only when they are completely ripe, or they will mildew or rot. The simplest way to find out is to give the gourd a slight twist. If it is ripe, it will come off the vine in your hand.

What to Do with Gourds at Frost Time

If your gourds are not ripe and frost is predicted, don't panic. Cut them off the vine, leaving a two-inch stem to prevent rotting, and put them in a warm, dry place.

How to Dry Gourds

There are so many marvelous things to be made from gourds that every gardener should grow them. You can make birdhouses, dippers, vases, and wall decorations, as well as table decorations. You can paint them any number of magnificent colors, but you've got to dry them before you do anything with them, and the way to do that is to hang them in a dry, airy place until they're very brittle. The skin, or rind, will become so hard you won't be able to dent it with a fingernail. If a mold forms while the gourds are drying, wipe it off with laundry bleach or rubbing alcohol. When a gourd is completely dry it will be not only hard, but very lightweight and hollow.

To make something out of it, draw a pencil line where you plan to cut, and use a keyhole saw to make the opening. You can cut the gourd before it is completely hard, but you run the risk of soft rot. It is easier to cut when it is not too hard, but you must sterilize the knife blade as a precaution against soft rot wherever you cut. When properly dried, a gourd will last a remarkably long time.

How to Make a Birdhouse from a Gourd

Cut your house by making an entrance hole for the size bird you want. Also drill a few holes in the bottom for drainage. Remove all seeds and fiber. Sand the outside carefully to make it nice and smooth, and then paint it. Just be sure everything is absolutely dry before you paint. You can use oil or latex paint.

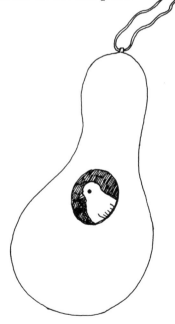

STRICTLY FOR THE BIRDS

Feeding Birds Is a Good Investment

Birds repay you for your generosity by eating the insects that eat your garden. Encourage them to stay around by feeding them. They'll use your feeder regularly, and in return they'll search your trees' bark crevices for wintering insects and insect eggs. Those are their quick snacks. Chickadees, creepers, nuthatches and woodpeckers especially should be encouraged.

Be an Instant Garden Expert

Did you know that a single plant of the weed purslane can produce a hundred thousand seeds? One plant, mind you. But hold your breath—one plant of lamb's-quarters produces a million seeds, and wormseed produces 26 million seeds! See why we need birds? Birds love those seeds. If they didn't, we'd be up to our you-know-what in seeds. So reward our feathered friends by feeding them in the winter, when their food is not very plentiful.

You May Not Be as Kind to the Birds as You Think

Birds are creatures of habit. Don't start feeding them in the winter unless you plan to continue. They come to depend on your daily handout and can starve if you stop. What you feed them is far more than they could get for themselves, and they get accustomed to a more generous amount of food. It's pure disaster when their food supply from you is cut off.

Make Your Birds a Christmas Present

Those little one-serving jelly containers you find in restaurants make marvelous dishes for birds and a great decoration for the tree at the same time. Empty out the jelly, then thread a string through the rolled lip of the container. Fill a lot of them with melted suet and bird seed and hang them on a tree. This is a marvelous work project for kids.

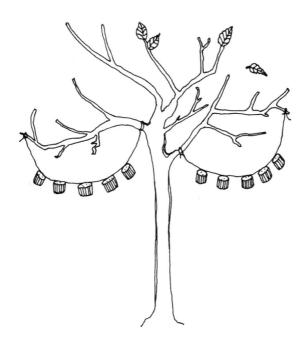

A Gourmet Recipe for the Birds

Melt suet and mix with peanut butter. The birds will love you for it. Pour the mixture into a plastic egg carton and tie it to a limb about seven feet off the ground so dogs and squirrels can't get at it.

When Peanut Butter Can Be Dangerous

It can choke birds if it isn't mixed with a little cornmeal or seed.

How to Get More Meat from Sunflower Seeds

Buy the smallest seeds. They have less hull and more meat. And that's what our fine feathered friends are looking for.

How to Keep Your Bird Bath from Freezing
(as Long as Possible)

Simply add a few drops of glycerine to the water. By the time it freezes, the birds won't want to take a bath anyway.

Where to Put the Door of a Birdhouse

Location is very important. The entrance hole should face the south because the coldest wind and the worst storms come from the north. Don't put your birdhouse up too high. Birds prefer heights of from 8 to 20 feet off the ground.

Something You Should Know About Wrens

They are the most fastidious of all birds. They're great housekeepers and keep their homes absolutely spotless. They will not move into a dirty house and will complain loudly if they find one.

Therefore, if you want to have them around, give them a clean, scrubbed-out, repaired and painted birdhouse. They'll keep it that way.

THE CHRISTMAS GREEN THAT ISN'T MONEY

How to Get Real Green in Your Christmas Greens

Cut your greens at Thanksgiving time instead of at Christmas. (When you cut them be sure you do it with the future shape of that tree in mind.) Soak the cut branches overnight in the sink or bathtub and then place them in plastic bags. Close tightly and store in a cool or cold place. At Christmas you will find them richer in color than if you had cut them that day.

Save Your Christmas Tree

Don't burn it. Let it dry, cut the branches into small pieces, and use them for mulch around acid plants such as blueberry, hydrangea and rhododendron. Use your neighbors' trees, too. They'll all love you for getting rid of their trees.

MAKE IT SPRING BEFORE NATURE DOES

How to Force Flowering Branches

Branches that flower indoors before winter is over can gladden the heart of anyone who sees them. Even a chronic grouch suddenly becomes almost human when there is a touch of spring in the air. For that reason, don't ever miss an opportunity to start spring a little early each year—indoors anyway. Cut flowering branches such as forsythia, crab apple, dogwood, pussy willow, flowering quince, spiraea, redbud, lilac, and azalea immediately after the buds begin to swell, and that's usually late winter. Split the stems three to four inches and put them in large containers of cold water in a dark room where the temperature runs from 65° to 70°. Drop a few pieces of charcoal into the water to keep it sweet, and change the water weekly. Every time you change the water, cut off about one inch of stem. Spray the branches with a fine mist of water at least twice a week; daily is better. As soon as the branches blossom, move them into bright sunshine to intensify their colors. To get different shades of color for an arrangement, move a few branches into the direct sunlight and keep the others in the shade.

Regulate Your Bloom

You can speed up forced blooms by splitting the branch stems three to four inches and placing them in hot water—about 100°. Do this once a day, allowing the branches to remain in the water while it's cooling. You can slow down blooming by keeping the branches in a cool, dark room.

 Frogs have it made. They eat what bugs them.

ELENA PIEROT

Chapter Eight

Miscellaneous Secrets

IF YOU CAN'T FIND IT
ANYWHERE ELSE,
LOOK HERE

USEFUL INFORMATION YOU NEVER
KNOW WHEN YOU'LL NEED

How to Bring Plants in from Foreign Countries

In order to import plants, you need a permit. The reason you need a permit is that the United States has quarantine restrictions to protect our plants from destructive foreign insects and plant diseases. Applications for permits to import plants should be sent to:

> Permit Unit
> USDA, APHIS, PPQ
> Federal Building, Rm. 638
> Hyattsville, Md. 20782

Be an Instant Garden Expert

Dazzle 'em with this kind of knowledge: so many botanical names of plants have two or more Latin words, such as *Achillea tomentose, Buxus sempervirens, Euonymus coloratus, Thymus vulgaris.* Don't be intimidated by them. The second word is often a description of the plant's habits, color, or manner of growth. Here's what some of the most frequently used ones mean: tomentosus—woolly; sempervirens—evergreen; coloratus—highly colored; vulgaris—common; alatus —winged; arborescens—treelike; cordatus—heart-shaped; hirsutus— hairy; humilis—small; speciosus—showy.

A Hedge in a Hurry

For a tall, fast-growing temporary hedge, plant castor bean (*Ricinus zanzibarensis*). It can grow as high as 13 feet in one season and is very showy when grown in a mass. Its large tropical leaves are quite spectacular and make a beautiful screen. The plants are toxic and the seeds are poisonous if eaten, but any area planted with castor bean is free from moles. This easy and inexpensive way to get a hedge in a hurry can be especially helpful when you've spent all your money for a new house and need some quick landscaping.

How to Move a Heavy Plant

Use your head, not your back. Move a heavy plant, tree, or anything else that's heavy by rolling it on sections of pipe. Use three or more pieces, depending on the size of what you want to move. Another way to move a heavy plant is to put it on your snow shovel and drag it along. This works best on a flat surface. Or if you have to move a heavy plant over smooth pavement, put it on a piece of burlap or canvas and then pull it.

How to Move an Evergreen Tree

Call an expert. However, if you're the daring type, try this. It certainly works well, but you have to start six months in advance for a good chance of success. It's called root pruning. Mark a circle around the tree. Make it two feet in diameter for trees up to four feet tall, three feet in diameter for trees up to seven or eight feet tall (I wouldn't attempt to move any larger ones). Now, take a sharp spade and cut around the circle, going as deep as you can through the roots. Next, pour liquid fertilizer into the soil where you have made your circular cut. The roots that have been pruned will be ravenous for food and in a few months will put out a profusion of new, fine roots which will be roughly in the shape of your circle. These pencil-thin roots will cushion the shock of transplanting and help the evergreen take to its new home.

Use Your Hose to Design a Curve

If you want to lay a new garden bed and want a curve in it, lay out your hose, tugging it here, pulling it there, moving it back and forth, until you've got the line you want. Then, with your spade, follow the line of the hose and dig a shallow trench. Perfection.

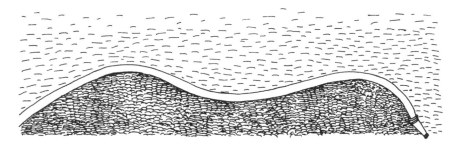

How to Keep Your Sprayer Unclogged

Sometimes powdered chemicals or organic mixtures don't completely dissolve in water and thus clog up your sprayer. To prevent this, stretch a nylon stocking over the mouth of the sprayer when you pour in your mixture. You'll be amazed at the amount of undissolved matter your strainer will catch.

How to Save Rainwater Cheaply

Remember the olde oaken bucket? That was what our great-grandparents saved rainwater in. Well, you just try to buy an old oaken bucket today, or a new one. It'll cost you. However, an oil drum can be bought at a reasonable price and can be used to catch and save rainwater. It has a plastic coating on the inside which is very resistant to rust, and if you use your charm on the salesman, he'll take off the top of the drum for you. Paint the outside of the drum if need be, and put a piece of screen over the top to keep out dunking birds and falling leaves. Then pray for rain.

If you need a lot of rainwater, cut short one of the downspouts on your house and place the oil drum under it so that it gets the water pouring off the roof.

How to Get Rid of Algae on Small Ponds

So many people tell me they get algae in the small decorative ponds they've built in their gardens. Often the reason is that the ponds are placed where the breezes can't get at them. A pond needs breezes, and the breezes have to be strong enough to cause rippling; otherwise the water is likely to get algae.

If your pond won't ripple, ripple it yourself with the help of some plastic and a tank-type vacuum cleaner. Simply cover the pond with a plastic sheet held down with stones, adjust your vacuum so it will blow instead of suck, insert the tube under the plastic, and you have made yourself a rippling breeze. Actually, you're providing a larger version of an aquarium aerator.

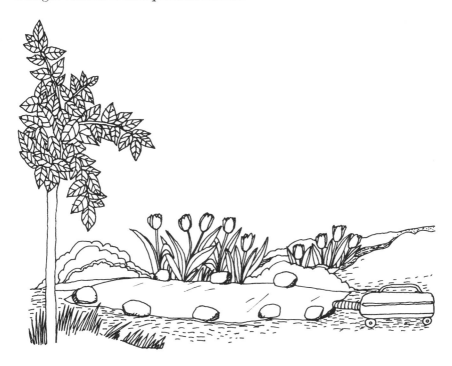

What You Should Know About Water Softeners

Never use water which has been artificially softened on your plants. It's too much of a risk: the sodium salts in artificially softened water can kill plants. And while I think of it, very hot or very cold water should also be avoided; otherwise your plants will be seriously shocked.

How to Stop Water from Seeping Through Garden Walls

If you have a dry-stack stone wall or one made of railroad ties, then you know how annoying those little gaps between the stones or ties can be when you're watering. The water goes through the holes rather than onto the plants. Well, here's a solution. It's called creeping thyme (*Thymus serpyllum*). It's a very low growing, sweet smelling herb with masses of roots which will take over and fill all holes and gaps, keep water out and look pretty, too. Thyme marches on!

Great Idea for Water Hyacinths

Water hyacinths are beautiful in a pond, but they spread too fast, sometimes taking over the entire pond or pool. Here's my secret for keeping them in check. Frame them. Make a wooden frame to form a square. You can make it any size, depending on the size of your pond or pool. I use one-by-twos, each a yard long, to form my square. I put an eye hook on the underside of each corner of the square, and I put a piece of wire through them and secure it. The other ends of the wires are twisted around a brick sitting on the bottom of the pool. The brick—you can also use a heavy stone—keeps the frame in one spot, and the frame keeps the water hyacinths together in one lovely, colorful mass.

Indian Remedy for Poison Ivy

The Indians brewed the roots and leaves of the jewelweed into a strong tea. It was said that a cupful would kill the poison-ivy infection, stop the itching and prevent future attacks. You're on your own if you try it. If in doubt, ask a friendly Indian.

Comfortable Steps

The same rules apply for garden steps as for those in your home. The riser of a step should never exceed 7 inches in height. The most comfortable tread-plus-riser measure is 18 inches.

Beauty Treatment for Hands While You Work

Here's a wonderful way to give your hands a "facial" while you're working in the garden. Get yourself some cheap nylon gloves. Rub a lot of Vaseline on your hands before you put these gloves on. If you're doing real grimy, heavy work, slip a heavier pair of regular gloves over the thin nylon ones. They'll protect your hands while they are getting their beauty treatment.

Nasturtiums and How to Eat Them

If you've never had a nasturtium in your salad or a nasturtium sandwich, you've missed tasting an exotic treat. Nasturtium blossoms as well as their leaves make fine eating. You can even stuff the flower with a mushroom or other hors d'oeuvre filling and serve it with cocktails. What a conversation piece it makes! Always wash the leaves and blossoms carefully if you're going to eat them.

Nasturtiums bloom well in full sun as well as in a northern exposure. They like poor soil and no fertilizer. When the soil is terrible and the food nonexistent, they give you more bloom and less foliage.

Nasturtium is a member of the cress family and gets its name from *nastus tortus,* which means "a convulsed nose," because of the plant's pungency.

Lilies Are for Eating

Day lilies—their buds, blossoms and flowers (if the flowers are not more than a day old)—make a delicious dish. Dip in batter and fry in sesame oil in a wok. Very Oriental, very good.

ODDBALL INFORMATION YOU NEVER KNOW WHEN YOU'LL NEED

How to Tell the Temperature Without a Thermometer

Crickets are natural thermometers. Some remarkable genius figured that you can tell the temperature by counting the number of chirps a cricket makes in a minute. Count them up, then subtract 40, divide by 4, and add 50. That's the temperature where the cricket is. You can do the same thing with katydids. Count the katydid chirps for one minute, subtract 19 and divide by 3. That's the temperature (Fahrenheit reading), courtesy of a katydid.

How to Make Jewelry from Corn

You won't find it at Tiffany's or Cartier's, but it's jewelry that's fun to wear, easy to make and low in cost. You make it from kernels of "calico corn," the very decorative and colorful corn you see in the vegetable departments around Thanksgiving time. Simply soak the kernels until they are soft, punch a hole in each one, and then string them with heavy nylon thread or an old fishing line. Dry them quickly, so they won't spoil, by placing them in a cool oven or leaving them on top of the refrigerator, which is always a warm place. Bracelets and necklaces made out of the corn are really spectacular. Be the first on your block to make them.

How to Make French Coffee from a Wildflower

With coffee prices the way they are, this secret could save you a bundle. Many people (especially the French) like a little chicory in their coffee. You can buy it, at a high price, from gourmet stores or fancy-food departments. You can also pick a substitute yourself in a field of wildflowers. It's the blue flower that we call cornflower. To make your own "chicory" brew, dig up the cornflowers to be sure you get the long taproot of the plant. Scrub the roots thoroughly and then roast them in a slow oven until they are hard and brittle and dark brown inside, which you will easily be able to see. Chop the roots very fine, or grind them if you have a coffee grinder, and use it as you would coffee.

Nasturtium for Ulcers

Did you know that nasturtium leaves can be used as a pepper substitute by people with ulcers and by those who must maintain salt-free diets? Just chop up the leaves very fine. You'll find it has a peppery flavor, and you won't have a need for salt if you use it.

THE GARDEN OF WEEDIN'

Some Kind Thoughts About Weeds

Some wise person called a weed a plant that interferes with the normal cultivation of another plant. One man's weed is another man's poison. As an example, if you were growing onions and discovered a zinnia in the onion patch, the zinnia would be considered a weed. There have been plenty of definitions of weeds: "a plant out of place," "an unloved plant," "a plant whose virtues have yet to be discovered." Don't knock weeds—many of our most beautiful flowers were once weeds. We're growing the improved strains in our formal gardens.

You Can Tell What Kind of Soil You've Got by Your Weeds

Weeds do have at least one virtue—they can show you the kind of soil you have. This knowledge is particularly useful if you're moving into a new home. If there is cinquefoil, selfheal or wild geranium growing in the soil, that means it's undernourished and needs a good application of fertilizer.

Your soil is acid if it has rabbit-foot clover, sorrel, or swamp horsetail growing wild in it. Your soil is alkaline if it has goldenrod, common spikeweed, salt grass, or pickleweed. If you see field mustard, horse nettle, morning glory, or quack grass, you'll find your soil is hardpan. Smartweed, beggar ticks, knotweed or meadow pink means that your soil has poor drainage. If you don't know what these weeds look like, get a good garden encyclopedia or go to your nearest garden store or nursery. Some of the companies that manufacture weed-destroying chemicals put out free booklets with pictures of the weeds.

Marvelous Way to Weed

Would you believe a pair of embroidery scissors and a six-inch-long pair of forceps are great tools for weeding? They are. And so are two small stools. Sitting on one of the stools, you can easily and comfortably snip off the heads of weeds which have just emerged with the embroidery scissors. If the weed is an old one, you use the forceps, grasping the weed at its base. A pull will take out the root and all. The forceps are also good for picking up insects you don't want to touch with your fingers—like slugs. The second stool? Well, that's for any friend who might drop in. She or he can sit on the stool while you talk. She or he can also help you weed while you talk —if you're smart enough to ask.

Quick Way to Get Rid of Weeds in the Walk

Those pesky weeds that spring up in sidewalk cracks can be disposed of by simply pouring hot salt water on them.

Terrific Plant to Grow Where You Sit, Swim or Eat

It's the tiny pennyroyal (*Mentha pulegium,* which means "bane of fleas"). This tiny mint grows horizontally and has a marvelous scent to humans, but the insects can't stand it. It's a perfect plant to have around your patio, swimming pool or eating area, or for growing between stones in a garden walk. It also has another very endearing quality. It doesn't mind being mowed.

How to Prevent Weeds from Springing Up in Sidewalk Cracks

If your sidewalk is in full sunlight, plant portulaca, preferably the new hybrids. They're larger than the ordinary portulaca, and their colors are clear and superb. Once started, they will certainly keep out the weeds and make your sidewalks glow with color. Really breathtaking. If you want to splurge, buy portulaca on seed tape. Then all you'll have to do is place the seeded tapes over the cracks, water, and stand back for a marvelous floral display where one would least expect it.

How to Grow Moss Between Stones

Here's another lovely way to keep out weeds between stepping stones or in sidewalk cracks. Grow moss. To start it, take a trip to the woods and look for moss with its little spore capsules starting to dry. Take the moss in sheets and dry it on a newspaper. When it's dry, rub the moss, spores and all, through a sieve to get it in powdered form. Then scrape the areas between your stepping stones or sidewalk segments with a stick, add a little sand, and then shake on the powdered moss. Keep it damp continually, not soaking wet but damp. In a year or two you'll have beautiful moss. (Lovely things like this do take a long while, but they are worth waiting for.)

What Dandelions Can Do for You

Dandelion is also known as the "potty" plant. In certain parts of the country it is known as "pee-a-bed" or "wet-a-bed," and in France it is known as *pissenlit,* which means just what you think it does, and for good reason. The dandelion stimulates your entire system, but in particular the kidneys and bladder. Wear your walking shoes when you drink delicious dandelion wine or tea.

Try This Unique Salad

Try dandelion greens in a salad. Pick the leaves when they are young and therefore tender. Not only do they taste good, but they are the best source of copper you can get. Try *salade de pissenlit* the way they serve it in France—a tangy salad of young dandelion leaves mixed with olive oil and a squeeze of lemon. *Bon appétit.*

Delicious Weed

Try chickweed in your salad. Very tasty.

Why Dandelions Should Be Dug Up

Take a good look at the dandelion the next time you dig it out of your lawn. It looks innocent enough—but what a thief it is. It robs the soil of its nutrients. It takes three times as much iron from the soil as any other plant. It also takes a good amount of copper and anything else it can lay its roots on. It depletes the soil so much that if it's not weeded out, it will stunt all the cultivated plants around it. Yet the dandelion is a paradox. Harmful though it may be to the soil when it's in the ground, it's very useful to the compost pile. Then it gives back all the iron, copper and other goodies it stole while alive.

How to Remove Weeds More Easily by Hand

If you don't want to use chemicals on your lawn to rid it of weeds, give the lawn a good soaking before you go out and weed it yourself by hand. You'll find the soaking makes the weeds more easily removable, even those with deep taproots, like dandelions.

How to Wash Your Clothes with Leaves

There isn't anything that Nature hasn't thought of first. For instance, did you know that the leaves of *Saponaria*, known also as soapwort, have been used for centuries by textile manufacturers for washing fine wools, linens and silks? *Saponaria*, which is really a weed these days, gets its name from the Latin word for soap (*sapo*), and for good reason. When the leaves are crushed, the pulp yields a soap-like lather, and it has been known to restore color and sheen to old and faded fabrics while it gives them a good cleaning. *Saponaria*, a member of the pink family, is often called "bouncing bet."

If you want to try your hand at restoring fabrics the way the museums do, here's how: tie quantities of the *Saponaria* leaves in cheesecloth or muslin bags and boil in soft water until foam appears and the water turns greenish. While the brew is brewing, soak the material to be cleaned in cold water so that much of the surface dirt is removed. Then lay the fabric on a board (over a bathtub, if possible), and with a sponge work the soapy froth in a circular motion over the surface—gently, of course. Continue with fresh foam until there is no longer any dirt left in the material. Then wipe the foam away and let the fabric dry in a cool and airy shaded location. *Saponaria* is hard to find, but it can be bought from Well-Sweep Farm, 317 Mt. Bethel Road, Port Murray, New Jersey 07865.

A Different (and Fantastic) Fertilizer

You won't believe it, but stinging nettles, those awful, irritating plants with hairy leaves and globular, sharp-pointed tips that pierce your skin and cling to your clothes, are absolutely fantastic in the compost pile. They're so good as a catalyst in fermenting the compost that they are used by commercial nurseries selling organic fertilizer. You can use them in your own pile or as a mulch around your plants, or, better still, make a complete plant food out of them by soaking them in rainwater for two or three weeks. Presto: a liquid fertilizer.

TAGS, TOOLS, TREES

Inexpensive and Permanent Plant Tags

Save your empty plastic bottles. Cut off the bottom and the top third of the bottle, and you'll have a thick piece of wonderful plastic to be cut into any size tags you want. Punch a hole in your tag, insert 24-gauge copper wire or a strip of old nylon stocking, and you're all set. Use an outdoor marker which is smearproof, waterproof and weatherproof.

Another Idea for Plant Tags

Here's another permanent tag that won't cost much, either. Buy a cheap green plastic tablecloth (not flannel-backed). Cut it into strips an inch wide and 8 inches long. Make an inch-long slit lengthwise at one end. Wrap the strip around the stem of a plant, insert the end of the tag into the slit, and pull it tautly around the stem.

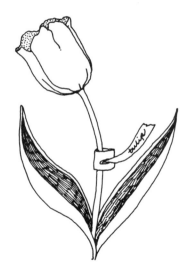

And Still Another

Save those styrofoam trays your supermarket meat comes in. Cut them to the label size you want and poke a hole at one end. If you don't have a waterproof pen, use a ball-point and write on the smooth side of the styrofoam. It's a little like embossing. When the rain washes out the ink, you'll still be able to read what you've written.

Fasten your labels with another freebie from the supermarket—those twist-'ems that come on bread sacks.

How Not to Lose Tools

Paint the handles of your garden tools red so you can always find them in the grass or soil. Why manufacturers of garden tools don't do that, I'll never know.

There's More to a Dead Tree Than Firewood

Why not be creative if you have to chop down a tree? Anybody can make firewood, but you can make rustic stepping stones or a garden seat for your garden path. For the "stones," slice the trunk into slabs, like a loaf of bread. To make a garden seat, cut the trunk lengthwise, join the halves at the back with hinges, and reinforce the joint with chains. Whether you make stepping stones or a garden seat, don't forget to use creosote to prevent rotting. Be careful when you use creosote; it can burn your skin.

Increase the Value of Your Home

Simply grow trees. That's not a joke. Beautiful trees on residential property can increase the value as much as 20 percent. Dr. Brian R. Payne, Forest Service environmental researcher at the University of Massachusetts, claims that the average increase in value of property when trees are planted is between 5 and 10 percent, which could mean a neat $3,000 to $6,000 jump in the average home's selling price. Do you suppose this is what they mean about money growing on trees?

Don't Blame the Dutch for Dutch Elm Disease

My Dutch husband will be happy and relieved to know that, contrary to popular belief, Dutch elm disease is not of Dutch origin, although it's gotten the Dutch in Dutch for years. The disease was first noticed in France, and the Dutch did investigate it. It then spread to Belgium, Holland, and the rest of Europe. There's no sure cure yet, but you can be sure they'll get one, and elms will once again bring elegance and grace to our streets and homes.

Be an Instant Garden Expert

Did you know that pine trees don't have pine cones when they are young? Just like us, they don't bear until they mature. Most don't bear cones until they are 15 or 20 years old. Some, no doubt precocious, bear when they are 10, while a few, such as the sugar pine of the west, seldom bear before they are 40 or 50 years old.

How to Get Pine Cones to Open When You Can't Wait for Nature

Take mature cones while they are green or light brown, and let them ripen in full sunshine. Cones will also open fully when placed in a warm oven for several minutes with the door open. Put aluminum foil on the bottom of the oven, because of the resin. And don't, *don't* close that oven door, or you'll be cleaning resin out of your oven for a long while. If the cones are very sticky with resin, leave them in the oven a while longer, and let it drip into an aluminum-foil pan.

How to Remove Pine Resin

When you work with pine cones or have to cut pine branches, you can't avoid getting the resin on your hands. Get rid of it with cleaning fluid—carbon tetrachloride—turpentine or alcohol, or lacking those, try ordinary nail-polish remover.

How to Get Rid of Stumps

A stump can be pulled out, chipped out, burned out or rotted out. Pull it out with a bulldozer, if you're rich. Chip it out with a stump axe, if you're energetic. Burn it out with gasoline, if you like to live dangerously. Or rot it out, if you've got patience and no money.

Rotting a stump takes a couple of years, but you weren't planning to hold your breath till it disappeared anyway. Cut off the stump at ground level or below. Cover it with soil and keep it moist. Nitrogen fertilizer, the kind you use on grass, will speed up the rotting process. Rotting can also be accelerated if you bore several holes in the stump before you cover it with soil.

How to Burn an Old Tree Stump Fairly Safely

First, bore holes in the stump about an inch in diameter and 6 inches deep. Drill them about 9 inches apart. Pour 2 ounces of potassium nitrate or sodium nitrate into each hole. Plug the holes with clay and leave them for 3 months. Then douse the top of the stump with charcoal-lighter fluid or jelly—the stuff that lights your outdoor grill—and ignite. This method is just great when the stump is old and dry, without any sap.

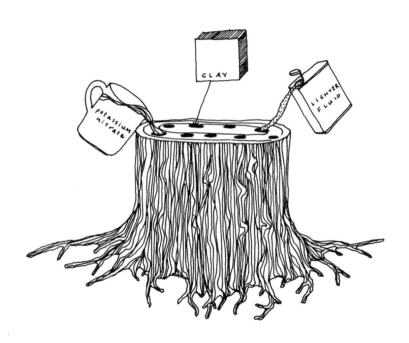

And Still Another

Plant Virginia creeper around the stump. Don't confuse Virginia creeper with Boston ivy. They are both in the same family, but Virginia creeper's leaves are divided into five fingers, while Boston ivy has three. Both have leaves which turn brilliantly scarlet in the fall.

Now that we have that straight, plant your Virginia creeper around the stump. It will cover the stump, and eventually it will make its way through the wood and destroy it. This is a slow but pretty way to get rid of a stump. Inasmuch as the vine spreads rampantly, all your nearby ground will be covered with it, so be careful where you plant it. But if it fits your spot, use it. It's lovely.

How to Get Tree Roots Out of Sewer Lines

This is a preventive measure and an inexpensive way to control roots. It's for use in porcelain toilets bowls only. (Never, *never* use it in a sink.) Pour one pound of quarter-inch crystals of copper sulfate into the toilet bowl. Agitate with a plunger before flushing to make sure all the crystals are carried down the drain so they can't damage or stain the porcelain. This treatment, twice a year, can control roots in tile sewer connections. There's evidently been no injury to trees or plants whose roots have been killed this way.

Since 1937 Ridgewood, New Jersey, has supplied copper sulfate to homeowners for killing roots in its sewer lines. The town stopped doing it for one year, and the cost of maintaining its sewer lines went up 40 percent. Needless to say, the town resumed the copper sulfate giveaway.

Tax Deduction

Trees lost because of violent wind, storm, fire or accident may be covered by your insurance, and if not, they may be tax-deductible if their loss reduces your property value. Check with your local IRS office.

Be an Instant Garden Expert

Did you know that dogwood was the wood the Greeks are reported to have used in building the Trojan horse? It made the Greek god Apollo very angry, because the wood was considered sacred. The cross Christ died on is purported to have been made of dogwood. The legend is that the dogwood was so ashamed of this that it never again grew large enough to be used for such a purpose. As if in penance, its bracts, which resemble a cross, bear the nail marks of the crucifixion at the tips, and its flowers forever blush pink in shame. I'm not sure I buy this legend—but it's interesting.

THE CRAWLING, FLYING UGLIES

How to Get Rid of Ticks

You or your dog can pick up ticks right out of the garden, but they will be easy to get rid of if you remember just one thing: when a tick enters a human's or dog's body, it screws itself in. The easiest way to get rid of it is to unscrew it. Hold the tick with a pair of tweezers and gently unscrew it in a counterclockwise direction.

Another Way to Nail a Tick

Another easy way to get rid of a dog tick is to put a tiny drop of fingernail polish on it. When the polish dries, the tick pulls its head out and suffocates. Then you can pluck it out without any fuss or bother.

How to Commit Murder and Be Thanked for It

If moths and mosquitoes bother you at night when you're sitting outdoors, put a shelf about one or two feet below the nearest light. Then fill a shallow pan with about two inches of water and pour a quarter of an inch of oil on the top. Put the pan on the shelf, and when the moths and mosquitoes and other night insects go after the light, they'll end up *down* in the water and oil.

A Nutty Way to Get Rid of Cat or Dog Fleas

Try to get a bagful of leaves from a black walnut tree if you live in an area where they grow. Spread the leaves, a lot of them, in the animal's sleeping area. In a few days the fleas will be gone.

Mint to Repel Mosquitoes

Pennyroyal (*Mentha pulegium*) is just fantastic for repelling mosquitoes. Its oil was a prime ingredient in old-fashioned mosquito repellents. Rubbing its leaves on your skin will discourage the biting pests. Try growing it around your patio or wherever you sit in your garden.

Instant Relief from Mosquito Bites

The fresh foliage of yarrow leaves, when crushed and rubbed over a mosquito bite, will remove the sting almost instantly. When you're eating out-of-doors, fill a vase with yarrow and dine in comfort. Well, almost.

The less help you have in your garden, the more it belongs to you.

CONNIE STONE

Index